Speaking Rather Seriously by William Pett Ridge

William Pett Ridge was born at Chartham, near Canterbury, Kent on 22nd April 1859.

His family's resources were certainly limited. His father was a railway porter, and his son, after schooling in Marden, Kent became a clerk in a railway clearing-house. The hours were long and arduous, but self-improvement was his goal. After working from nine until seven o'clock he attended evening classes at Birkbeck Literary and Scientific Institute and then he would write.

From 1891 his humourous sketches were published in the St James's Gazette, the Idler, Windsor Magazine and other literary periodicals of the day. He was heavily influenced by Dickens and critics thought he might be his successor.

Pett Ridge published his first novel in 1895, A Clever Wife. By his fifth novel, Mord Em'ly, three years later, his success was obvious. His writing was written from the perspective of those born with no privilege and relied on talent to find humour and sympathy in his portrayal of working class life.

Today Pett Ridge and other East End novelists including Arthur Nevinson, Arthur Morrison & Edwin Pugh are grouped together as the Cockney Novelists.

With his success Pett Ridge gave generously of both time and money to charity. In 1907 he founded the Babies Home at Hoxton, one of several children's organisations

His circle considered Pett Ridge to be one of life's natural bachelors. In 1909 they were rather surprised therefore when he married Olga Hentschel.

As the 1920's arrived Pett Ridge added to his popularity with the movies. Four of his books were adapted into films.

Pett Ridge now found the peak of his fame had passed. He still managed to produce a book a year but was falling out of fashion and favour with the reading public. His canon runs to over sixty novels and short-story collections as well as many pieces for magazines and periodicals.

William Pett Ridge died, on 29th September 1930, at his home, Ampthill Willow Grove, Chislehurst, at the age of 71.

Index of Contents

PREFACE

In this volume there is no attempt to climb mountains; heroic reformers, content with nothing less than endeavours to scale lofty mountains, may express the opinion that I am only going up Primrose Hill, and it is true my references are mainly restricted to London.

London, however, is not so even of surface or so easy for travelling as some imagine, and my work having made me acquainted with certain of the obstructions which interfere with straight progress, I offer, in the following pages, certain recommendations.

W. Pett Ridge.

THE RECRUITING SYSTEM

The system always owed much to illumination, and with streets furnished by electric light, the power of attracting is not diminished. Even the Londoner finds himself at times startled by the brilliant evening appearance of some jeweller's shop anxious to give to its contents all the assistance that powerful globes can contribute, and reckless concerning the quarterly account; the Londoner may ascertain, with the aid of multiplication table, the effect these dazzling lights have upon the countryman. Up for the day, the youth from Surrey makes comparison between all this and the dark, lonesome road which he will find upon his return immediately after leaving the few oil-lamps of Milford Station, and his mind becomes made up either with celerity or with deliberation, according to the speed at which it is able to move. Immigration from country to town would be greater, but for the ingenious arrangement of holding the Cattle Show at Islington in the early days of a month that provides fogs; all recruiting influences are of no avail in these circumstances, and the country lad goes back to report London as an over-rated town, to announce Milford is good enough for him.

The youth who, seeing town under more favourable lighting, gives in to its attractions, is welcomed by certain forces, as one adding to the strength of the regiment. His intelligence in early days may not be of a high order, but a little practice improves in this regard; his appearance lacks something of smartness, but he is sufficiently imitative to remedy details, and a year or two sees him wearing the most advanced collars, becoming something of an authority in regard to neckties. These satisfactory results occur only when procedure from the outset is well and wisely planned. The lad, for instance, who enters the service of a railway company or joins one of the large wholesale firms in the City, will find that improvement and promotion come, not swiftly or as from the influence of a fairy wand, but in a regular, deliberate annual way, providing he does his work in a satisfactory manner.

Superlative genius is not expected from him; amazing intelligence is not looked for; his employers are satisfied if day in and day out he gives capable services. He enjoys (or suffers from) a tremendous appetite, and the landlady who undertakes to provide him with board and lodging for fifteen shillings a week, reckons herself fortunate if she does not lose over the transaction. In domestic service, also, as groom or footman, he may find his place and keep it; to him we are principally indebted for the attention given across shop counters.

It is when he comes to London with no fixed intentions regarding the career to be pursued there, and when on arriving at the terminus he cannot claim a useful relative or a helping friend, that his case, from the very outset, becomes parlous, and his life resembles that of a stray dog. I have met him, three months after the day on which he stepped out of the uptrain, waiting outside the dock gates in the early hours. I have met him within six months at a Salvation Army shelter. The velocity of his descent receives no check when he happens to be too shy to call for help, and he adds himself speedily to the mingled collection of human beings huddled so closely together and so much disabled by the fall, that they seem to have no great desire either to pick themselves up or to allow anyone else to assist.

Can this be altered? I, a countryman, feel acutely for the disabilities under which the immigrant may spend his first days in town. It happened in my own case that I made friends immediately, and the friends I made then are my friends to-day. But it is easy to imagine the case of a new arrival who, not favoured by early incidents, or without the effrontery to make acquaintances, walks about London, his loneliness emphasised and increased in noting the friendly relations enjoyed by other people. For him, there must be black tragic hours ere he reaches the hopeless stage.

The Londoner born, starting under adverse conditions and never rising above them, lives, at any rate, in a world and in a town to which he has always been accustomed, and if one could look at the situation from the back of his head, one would probably find he has fewer grievances than might be expected; fewer indeed than he should possess. But when to that stratum of London the country-bred is forced to add himself, thoughts must, many a time, go back from narrow streets, noisy tenement dwellings and drab environments to his own village with its peace and its fresh, clean air, and God's own sky, broad and wide above.

If the Church did all it might, if chapels had more generous arms, and if high authorities did not resent ambition in any but themselves, no youngster would leave a country village without an invoice. A lifeless hare sent up to London bears an addressed label with a parcels ticket carefully pasted on the reverse side, and a waybill giving destination and all particulars; if the hare should go astray on the journey, immediate inquiries are made and efforts to trace it at once instituted. A young man may take a ticket at a country station to travel by the same train with but little more idea of his destination than the lifeless hare possesses; at the terminus, whilst the hare will be met by a porter who takes it to the Up Parcels

Office, where arrangements are made for its prompt and safe delivery, the youth steps out to receive no attention except from the official at the barrier who collects his ticket.

Is there not enough wisdom and good nature in the world to form a better system? I should like to see a method of procedure extended on the lines of a society that exists for showing friendliness to young female servants. No lad, leaving a country village without the certainty of a position waiting for him in town, should go without a notice being sent to the head office where arrangements would be made for him to be met and conducted to a decent place of repose, and for the registering of his name and qualifications.

All very well to deride the grandmotherly manner, but the grandmotherly manner will be necessary so long as there are people whose bodies only have grown up. For the truth is, those of us born in the country are, in our youth, so inexperienced in the art of conversation, that on coming to town we feel something of the nervousness of a man making an after-dinner speech for the first time, and unable to conceal astonishment and fear at the sound of his own voice. This is the moment when friends are wanted; so earnestly, in fact, that any hand held out is grasped without regard to the owner. In the case of many, the hand belongs to an institution like the Birkbeck College, or the City of London College, or one of the Polytechnics, and the lad is safe.

But I have in my mind the youth who comes from the farm with no desire for education, some desire for entertainment, a very real desire for company. I believe the county associations which exist in London, from the one representing Kent to the one representing Aberdeenshire, would be ready to find responsible men and women to carry out the scheme, and I am certain that there are many ways by which those possessing wealth and good nature could disburse either or both to less advantage. One likes to hear a provincial accent by day among sturdy City constables; it is not so pleasing to hear it at night on the seats of the Embankment. Never a laugh, mark you, comes from the Embankment at night.

THE LAUGH OF A CHILD

Few things are so unimpressive to general eyes—I myself possess quite an ordinary pair—as the exhibition of figures; and when I have said that in London there are threequarters of a million of youngsters educated at the expense of London and of the nation, and costing five million pounds a year, the statistics in this article begin and end. For which reason I ask you to look at them again and make a determined endeavour to realise their importance.

Seven hundred and fifty thousand children; disbursements, £5,000,000 per annum.

Most people have limits to their mathematical imaginings, and once these are reached a few noughts more make but little difference; so that they give the same air of surprise, the eyebrows go up to the same height, whether one talks in hundreds or in billions. I find in my own case that I can endure a slight shower; but when figures are rained down upon me furiously, I am forced to open my umbrella as a means of protection, turn up the collar of my overcoat, perhaps find disguise in a mackintosh, and cry "Tell me not in mournful numbers." The fire of interest in public affairs rarely bums so determinedly that it cannot be put out by a douche of this kind, and as my desire is to fan and to encourage it I content myself by repeating—three-quarters of a million boys and girls, interned from nine to twelve of a morning, and two to half-past four of an afternoon; five millions of pounds taken out of the public purse every year. For this money we get a good deal.

The youngsters, leaving school at the age of fourteen, have learnt something like obedience to commands, a fair knowledge of the past history of their country, and (excepting amongst the incredulous) a good idea of how the land lies and where the seas exist. They have ascertained that no great discomfort exists in the possession of clean hands and a well-washed face. This is good; some have been taught to swim, which is better. It has been borne in upon them that the best way in walking is to keep chin up and shoulders well back. They possess a handwriting which, but for a certain laboriousness of manner, compares favourably with that adopted by some of us, reckoned amongst the mature, since it permits itself to be read; too often with the penmanship of authors (for instance) one has to toss up a coin to decide whether a word is Wednesday or Winchelsea.

These are qualifications counting for success and comfort and serenity, and the generous mind may fed they are not dear at the price to which reference has been made. My view is not from the point of those who pare cheese, and I am not going to grumble at the cost. What I desire is the omission of one study, and the substitution of a Class for Laughter.

A Bishop, who has the rare and peculiar gift of goading me into violent opposition whenever we meet on public platforms (he pretends the fault is his, and I allege the fault to be mine, but neither of us believes the other; we always part good friends, at any rate, he does), once said that the laugh of the London factory girl was something of which the hyena would be ashamed. I hope I was right in pointing out that wonder ought not to be exhibited at the quality of her laugh; amazement had to be reserved for the fact that she laughed at all. I also remarked that if she had in early days opportunities for practice she would perhaps rival the silvery cadences, the rippling notes, the gay intonations notoriously adopted by Bishops and other high dignitaries in expressing amusement. This was sheer ill-nature and spleen on my part, but there are moments when nothing short of a powerful anaesthetic will stop one from discarding good manners. All the same—forgiveness is here begged for the sin of bragging—there was, somewhere concealed in this, a small nugget of truth.

Not one penny of the five millions of pounds annually disbursed goes to the teaching of Laughter. All the child has in this direction comes from natural instinct, and the natural instinct of a child is to laugh only at the disasters of other people. I have found this to exist in otherwise staid and sedate adults, to such a degree that a severe accident to a dose personal friend sends them into a state of delight, landing them on the very edge of hysteria. In any playground of the County Council schools you may find minutes go by with plenty of noise, any amount of shrieking, and a profusion of argument; when at last a scream of laughter comes you can be sure that some one, by inadvertence, has received grievous injury. In children's hospitals, when entertainments are given. Punch and Judy shows are the safest and the surest, because no baby in the ward is so small or so ill that diversion cannot be extorted when the policeman is knocked down. During the brief space given up to harlequinades in the pantomime season, all the signs of amusement come from children in the house when adult persons are encountering, as a result of clown's ingenious preparations, personal hurt; the while parents are discussing such matters, relatively unimportant, as the earliest possible train to be caught from Charing Cross.

Something can be done and should be done to accustom the youngsters in the County Council schools to the sound of their own laugh, and the task would not be difficult. It fortunately happens that in England all the successful humorous writers—I hope it is superfluous to say that no one can count the present scribe amongst them; I wish they could—the successful humorous writers have pens that are never dipped into anything but good, decent ink. To read their works is to illuminate and brighten the mind; not to corrupt. If trouble be found in making a selection amongst the modems, there are many writers of the past—a large bouquet from which any flower can be taken, and the cautious pruning to which 3ome classics have to be subjected will not be found necessary. I have heard children on certain afternoons reciting stolidly cut-off lengths of Shakespeare, one half of which they do not comprehend and the other half of which they ought not to understand, and I do believe they would be better employed in the direction I have indicated. The superstition to be overcome—its size and importance have been reduced of late years—is that to laugh heartily betokens the empty mind. So far as my experience goes, the keenest sense of humour is possessed by men and women whose minds are admirably furnished, and if these do not always express themselves loudly it is because of a polite desire to refrain from astonishing neighbours. The point is that one should learn to laugh in early days, when life is new and amazing and possesses many of the qualities of a joke; the study becomes hard for those who have neglected it in the hours of youth, and their efforts give opportunities for criticism from Bishops.

For the well-to-do, whose incomes do not compel them to stop when necessaries are obtained, but can adventure at any moment into luxuries, there exists no sort of difficulty, for they make a demand just as in the days beyond recall a lord flicked finger and thumb and called upon the paid fool of the household to divert an over-fed company. This evening, or any evening, the well-to-do take their choice of a thousand jesters ready to exert themselves to the last point in order to raise a smile, and the well-to-do count half a guinea soundly invested if, as a result, they are enabled to relax for a moment the stolidity of their manner. On these folk I do not squander my interest, although at times there is a temptation to extend to the over-amused the sympathy one gives to those for whom no amusement exists. I ask for on6 hour a week from the time given by the State to education, in which hour the youngsters may hear themselves laugh.

It would be almost as grateful to them as food.

A VICTORIAN REVIVAL

London varies its changes in various ways. Sometimes violently, as when one side of a narrow street is suddenly plastered with forbidding notices, shutters go up, protecting hoardings are fixed, men with pick and shovel stand perilously on the roof, dislodging bricks; before the passers-by have time to get the dust out of their eyes, the road is broadened and new shops being built. Sometimes casually, as when a custom that has been under one's observation for many years dwindles slowly, and on vanishing the final difference is so small that you can easily believe it never existed in the large; only when some one returns after a considerable holiday and makes inquiry in regard to the custom do you detect the fact of its disappearance. I tell you, London is ever playing tricks of this kind. Two eyes and two ears are not enough in the way of furniture for anyone who desires to miss nothing that goes on, or goes off, in the big town.

For instance, those of us who cannot plead the excuse of youth ought not to have forgotten a solemn rite of Sunday mornings when processions walked through the minor streets on the way, bearing carefully a covered plate or tin, depositing these at a place agreed upon; returning two hours later to regain the baked meat-offerings and carry them now with even greater solicitude than before, although driven to increased haste by reason of burnt fingers, reaching home with the contents hissing and spluttering excitedly, there to be welcomed by shouts of—

"Here's dinner come at last!"

Usually the eldest girl of the family found herself entrusted with the important duty; a prejudice against giving the task to a boy was due, I fear, to the ugly suspicion that he could not avoid taking samples on the return journey and making tests of well-done comers of the joint. Here was probably one of the instances where the many had to suffer for delinquencies of the few. The supply of girls in families is still adequate, and I ask whether there is any reason why this excellent old custom should not be restored. It is almost extinct.

Those who have taken off the roofs of houses where dwell the folk counted below the middle-class, and have peeped in, do not need to be told that a large half of the trouble, physical and mental, to be found there is due to imperfect cooking. The subject can only be argued under shelter of the printed word, for a woman may confess to many faults, but will stubbornly refuse to admit that any defect can be justly found in her powers of preparing food for the table. Here, in print, it is possible to say, and it is absolutely correct to declare, that to ninety per cent. of the domestic managers of the class referred to, the precise moment for withdrawing a steak from the attentions of the fire is unknown, the time to be given for the boiling of vegetables is determined only by the arrival of the hour of one.

To partake of meat prepared under such conditions induces a man to become a vegetarian; to eat the vegetables forces him to become a flesh-eater; in the confusion of thought thus engendered, one path only appears dear and obvious, and that path leads to the public-house. There at any rate, he will find cheerful company, animated conversation, fairly good spirits. And to that haven, after a meal of under-done pork, overdone pudding, and a few hard potatoes that might be used as implements of warfare, he accordingly goes. I don't blame him, and I certainly cannot blame the public-house for taking his money, but I do wish the excuse for his visits could be reduced. I see nothing for it but the creation, in districts where they are required, of a system of ranges and cooks.

You will remember that even where, in the tenement dwellings, ability is found, the means of cooking a meal are inadequate. If gas-stoves are not fixed, the expense of making up a sufficient fire constitutes a serious addition to the expenses; no one pays so dearly for coals as the hard-up Londoner, and too often the merchant, by error, supplies an article better fitted for the repairing of housetops. Not alone in this particular does the hard-up Londoner pay extravagantly.

For her, to all intents and purposes the duty on tea has never been reduced, in that the small quantities she buys are mainly composed of dust; for her, nearly every article purchased at the small general shop is weighed with a carelessness that rarely errs in her favour.

The supreme blunder is committed at the butchers' stalls. A market penny will not go far, I know, but it ought never to start in the direction of the almost useless remnants which she considers there. Small wonder that when she takes her selection home, she feels puzzled to know how to deal with it. A chef at a one and three penny restaurant in Little Compton Street would find a way, thanks to impudence and sauce, but she has neither, and when the dish appears on the table and criticisms begin at the first mouthful, the dispirited lady can only remark.

"Well, it was the best I could do with it!"

You will not forget that, with these folk, Sunday dinner is the event of the week, something to be looked forward to with relish, something which should provide food for retrospection. In other circles, I find stout and well-fed people bragging of abstinence, but this, upon inquiry, proves to be only the refusal of potatoes or a steadfast resolution to take toast in lieu of bread. Here the aspiration is, that on this one day of the week, it will be possible to slightly over-eat. Considering the rarity of the event, this would be pardonable; it might not be hurtful if the food were well-cooked, but the imagination is staggered when one thinks of the results under present arrangements.

The cookery centres will reckon in favour of coming generations, but with women's increasing determination to work and to earn a living, the finer arts of domesticity cannot be cultivated. At present, many a factory girl marries a working-man and sets upon household duties with nothing more dear in her mind than the impression that a chop should be fried for three minutes and a half. On behalf of cases of this nature I make my suggestion. If it is objected that Sunday work will be increased, the answer is that one capable man or woman can superintend the effective cooking of forty dinners, and unless my mental arithmetic has become grievously at fault, this means not an increase but a decrease in Sunday labour. The old charge, I am told, was twopence; a fair sum. Voluntary associations or borough councils could select a bakery, or a small restaurant—free for the morning from other occupations—and if necessary, provide at first a small subsidy. Everything would be over and cleared away by one o'clock. The time at present given by the wife to unsatisfactory culinary experiments could be devoted to the tidying of rooms and to domestic duties now deferred until later in the day, the afternoon would be free for the parks; it is just possible that the idea of going to church or chapel might be seriously entertained.

I know these people, and I believe, after a good many years of watching, I can appreciate some of the difficulties of their lives. They are, in many ways, mere children in their incapacity to move out of the ruts which have been made for them, but a great deal can be done by holding out, without any pretence of pity, useful assistance. Large reforms, requiring platform speeches and Bills that are reluctant to turn themselves into Acts, can be left to those who enjoy the handling of stupendous operations, but there are some alterations which can be effected without reckless expenditure of words, or drawing up of deeds; here is one of a size, that has no regard to its importance, to which I beg your consideration. The prospect of a well-cooked meal might even induce the Londoner to gain an appetite by the desperate means of taking exercise in the parks.

OUTDOOR MOVEMENTS

The temper of Londoners is regulated by the amount of exercise they take. Policemen are, for the most part, good humoured; postmen are brisk and independent; lamplighters remaining in the suburbs whistle as they go, out of sheer exhilaration of spirits; railway porters who do platform work form the most cheerful body of men, excepting in foggy weather.

On the other hand, cabdrivers are so morose that certain of them can only say "Thank you" when under the influence of a double fare and laughing gas; tailors, cobblers and others who similarly go through the days without walking, form a political party of their own, finding the opinions in "Reynolds's" all too mild. One can feel every desire to see the means of transport extended and improved, and at the same time recognise that the more London rides, the worse its temper will become. Unless the town takes care to give itself compensation for the decrease in forced marches, it will arrive at the contentious stage to be found near the rank in Adelaide Street, Strand. In a desire to arrest this movement I call the attention of Londoners to the existence of parks and open spaces.

To the majority these are mere geographical expressions. I have heard on the North side of the river some of the very people who should live half of their lives in the open air speak of Hampstead Heath as though it were an unattainable point which several had endeavoured to reach, perishing in the gallant attempt and leaving their poor bodies to bleach in Kentish Town Road.

An old lady of my acquaintance who resides in some model dwellings near St Pancras Station, and has resided in that borough all her life, told me the other day that she had often resolved to take the devil by the horns and see what Regent's Park was like; she had not yet given up the hope of making some day this heroic, desperate, ten minutes' expedition. I offered to escort her by omnibus; she replied that there was no occasion for hurry. Concerning Hyde Park, the general impression in many quarters seems that it is reserved for political demonstrations, and that good form would be infringed if one entered near the Marble Arch unaccompanied by a violently-coloured and fiercely emblazoned banner.

Haverstock Hill, a gentle ascent, has the reputation fairly possessed by the Wetterhorn; Highgate is a spot to which it is correct to go only in a conveyance led by black horses. Of Finsbury Park, the fear, that is almost a hope, seems to be that it was surely built over long ago. Victoria Park is too new; Greenwich Park too old. Blackheath is considered draughty, whilst at Peckham Rye one may encounter Tom, Dick, and Harry. Similarly, Kennington Park and Clapham Common are the resort of the tag, rag and bob-tail. You will observe that no Londoner is so indolent as to be unwilling to take the trouble of finding some excuse for not taking trouble.

Only fair to say that those who manage London have made admirable efforts in the past few years to induce folk to taste the joys of fresh air. The bands have drawn to open spaces young couples who would otherwise lounge aimlessly about the streets; it has been even more satisfactory to see mother bringing the children to listen; father joining the party alter he has had time to wash and put on a dean collar. The cheap programmes contribute to their musical education, and no young man can now afford to make the general guess, when challenged to give a title, that it is something or other out of " Faust."

In most of the parks, but not in all, one can manage to obtain certain refreshments; I wish it were likely that prejudice could be so far overcome as to permit father on a summer evening to obtain his glass of beer without hurrying the entire party away and through the gates into the main road. A rather nervous effort has been made to set up newspaper kiosks. In some corners, provision has been made for mature men who are not so mature but that they can unbend in public to play bowls. You can always tell when you are nearing the lawn tennis portion by the ejaculations from young Ladies of—

"Oh, bother!"

"I am a silly!" And other self-reproachful comments.

It will scarcely be pretended that because something has been done, nothing remains to be done. A good deal remains to be done. I should like to see folk introduced to the parks, folk who would benefit considerably by the acquaintance; the loafers who at present sleep there by day might well be ejected, in order to give room for new-comers. District visiting is undertaken by many admirable people; I wish these would learn the use of the lasso and carry away at a run the women on whom they call, together with needlework, to spend an hour or two in the nearest park. I wish that on afternoons when schoolrooms become unbearable and little youngsters have difficulty in keeping eyes open, and teachers cannot keep eyes from the dock, that they could give up books and be taken off—this is being done in a partial manner—to sit on the grass, learn the names of trees and flowers, and try to understand something of the wonderful world into which they have been born.

I wish that the flowers in the parks, just before they begin to fade and when their successors are being prepared, could be cut and presented in bunches to the schools in the hard-up districts. I wish the authorities of the Botanical Gardens would lend me the beautiful space under their control and allow me to take there on a few August Saturdays—when the members are, or ought to be, away from town— a thousand youngsters from Somers Town and Lisson Grove; I would be mother, and provide tea, and pour it out.

I wish that on Saturdays also the fine squares in Bloomsbury and elsewhere were free to children who gave a guarantee of behaviour. I wish Somers Town recognised that for three pence it could go and 'return by tram-car, spending hours in delightful surroundings, with a view on the north side going away to Harrow, and on the south a picture of the amazing town in which Little Clarendon Street and Park Lane are situated.

Astonishing to find how parochial the Londoner can be. For many, bridges across the river do not exist. The tube railways offer services, but Dalston still regards Lewisham with distant contempt, and what Lewisham thinks of Dalston had better not be recorded. Where the Londoner lives, is the only spot he can look upon as reasonable. In the old farce, visitors from South London expressed this very accurately. "Grosvenor Gardens?" they cried. "Do you mean to say you live in such an out-of-the-way comer as Grosvenor Gardens? Why don't you live somewhere central, like Brixton?" It is this feeling of disdain that prevents the Londoner from making explorations, stops him from appreciating the green spaces, possession of which would make any other town proud and conceited. One of the results can be found in the circumstance that a Sunday afternoon in the London parks affords good opportunities for those who wish to pick up foreign languages. The worst immigrant has defects, but it can be claimed for him that he knows a good park when he sees it, and for the time, at any rate, he is breaking no law.

TO FIT THE CRIME

Others beside Mr Labouchere find a relish in criticising the inflictions made by those who administer the law. Most people in reading columns devoted in the journals to police courts and other courts of law, where the more important cases are decided, make up their minds as they follow the case, anticipating the verdict and presently expressing approval, dismay, or a grudging assent which hints pretty broadly that they—if entrusted with the duties—would have judged more wisely. I am told few occurrences fill an editor's letter-box so completely as an obviously harsh decision, one that arouses the sentiment of people; where money is required by the distressed parties, it generally happens that a definite announcement has to be made in order to arrest the deluge of benevolence.

A judge of the High Courts after giving whole days to the hearing of a case, being assisted by tolerably wakeful jurymen and illumination on both sides by counsel, sums up carefully, and the evening papers rush into the streets announcing the result. An hour later at Muswell Hill, at Blackheath, at Brondesbury, at Kew, furious pens are spluttering and a wife who, on being appealed to, cannot tell the writer on the instant how to spell the word "travesty," finds some of the blame sent in her direction. Unhampered by exact reports, and free from the prejudice created by having witnesses under personal observation, the writers are able to take sides without any delay; the only point which requires thought being in the selection of a pen-name. Shall it be "Senex," or "Pater," or "Jeunesse," or "Fiat Justitia"?

In something of a like spirit, and in the same desire to act as Court of Appeal, I want to suggest that the weights in the scales of justice should be slightly altered, without, however, affecting the balance to any great extent. It seems to me—difficult to avoid using the old debating society phrase—it seems to me that some should be made lighter and others should be heavier. The latest figures I have been able to see report that offences against property have increased, whilst offences of violence show diminution, and one is tempted to look upon this as a satisfactory tendency. The only offence against the person which shows an added number is bigamy, and somehow this is a crime that includes an element of the ludicrous; there certainly appears in most cases of the kind to be more of fatuousness than anything else. Concerning offence against property, this may not, strictly speaking, be cricket, but it is in many respects very like the game, excepting that the odds are the odds of one man playing against several teams. (The proportion is actually as 177 to 100,000.)

I, representing the side called Property and having for my opponent Crime, possess the advantage of being supported—apart from my own ingenuity—by others who are sympathetic, by members of the police force, by neighbours on either side, by every magistrate and judge in the land. If Crime, playing almost single-handed, contrives in these circumstances to score and to beat me, I may well feel abashed by the incident, but the instincts of sport should prevent me from feeling revengeful; having discovered how he managed to defeat me, all I have to do is to see that in the next contest I take care not to give him again the same opportunity.

As for instance. A man walking in Notting Dale on a summer's evening, his jacket unbuttoned and displaying a gold watch-chain, looks down and discovers that of this decorative article but a mere remnant is in his possession; the rest of the chain, and the whole of the watch have gone. What he usually does is to scream "Stop thief!" and to arrest and hold the first plain-clothes detective who hurries up in his direction; the next morning he sends a minatory letter to New Scotland Yard, hinting that the Chief Commissioner had better resign. In effect, he has only been gently reproved for his own carelessness, and the course for him to adopt is, in future, to leave his watch at home when visiting Notting Dale, or to keep jacket buttoned, and to see that a chain does not issue invitations.

The proverb concerning the uselessness of locking the stable door alter the horse is stolen, contains very little truth and, looked on as a piece of advice, may be counted as of no value. The right course to pursue is to benefit by experience, buy another horse, and also make a purchase at the establishment of Messrs Chubb. If the taker of the horse can be found he should certainly be compelled to restore it with a suitable apology, and the owner, on his side, might well express regret that he, by carelessness, exposed the other to temptation; a reasonable arrangement would be to punish both for conspiracy. Should the taker of the horse get the animal away, he now represents Property, and has to endure the drawbacks of his new position. The most indignant man I ever met was an acquaintance of mine, living in Huntingdon Street, Hoxton, whose house was one night entered and robbed of articles which he himself had acquired by means other than purchase.

But the leniency which I would like to see presented to those who desire the property belonging to neighbours—a task on which all of us are engaged, either in a profession, or a trade—can be compensated by increased severity in regard to offences of violence. One may look with equanimity on the action referred to in Notting Dale, but it becomes a different matter when Notting Dale knocks the possessor of the watch on the head, or clutches his arms from behind. These are acts of superfluous naughtiness, and must be checked. You, doing no hurt to the body of people, have a right to expect the same treatment, and possess a good excuse for resenting deeply any infraction of this law of good manners.

The more necessary to punish offences of the kind, and to punish them sharply, because it is scarcely possible to make a perfect system of defence. Your property can be guarded, or placed in strong rooms, but you are compelled to take your body with you wherever you walk. In days of very long ago, when more freedom existed in regard to personal attack, men wore coats of mail and vizors, and adopted other means of protection; if one can trust the historical novel, they also possessed a wonderful facility for recovering from wounds, so that an ugly stab in the shoulder left them with nothing worse on the following morning than a slight stiffness. To-day, under the care of experienced doctors, a similar injury remains for weeks, and then leaves one open to the most recently invented complaints.

For this reason, whilst imbued with friendliness towards Notting Dale, and recognising the many difficulties that must be encountered by a man anxious to make a dishonest living, I cannot look with toleration on his attempts to strike peaceable folk on the head, or to administer other forms of maltreatment. He must not do it. He must not attempt to do it. If these words of mine fail to impress him, I look to magistrates and others administering the law to make the argument more definite, and should he be so stubborn as to decline to see that I have reason on my side, then, in the last resource, he must be hauled out of the down trains and a request made to a muscular warder and to a cat of at least nine tails.

THE DOWN TRAINS

One of the few pictures which will always remain in my memory—most of them become scraped out and are replaced by more convincing scenes of actual life—was in the rooms of the Institute a few years since. It gave as the centre figure a hopeless, helpless, male loafer on one of the wooden seats of the Embankment; at the side, two smartly dressed women rustled by; the title (the grim part of the whole idea) "Nothing to Sell." I remember some of the critics were greatly shocked and, approving the quality, technique and other virtues that I only dimly understand, reproved the artist in severe Auntie-Emma phrases for his choice of subject. I think I did comprehend the meaning of the artist; I think he intended to compare the life of the indolent woman with the life of the lazy man. In all fairness, it is as well to remember this in considering the fact that the lowest regiment is constantly being recruited by men who originally belonged to a crack corps and have come down by easy descent because (according to themselves) they have never had luck; because (according to their friends) they have made no effort to succeed. The number of these can be judged even by folk who do not go into the depths to meet them, by recalling that there are not many families of one's acquaintance but where some member is absent, some name never mentioned. Only a quiet funeral at Highgate—no flowers, by request—restores the name to the list, and permits the children to speak of the detrimental relation. And those who, from their heights, take a disdainful view of the bed-rock of society—

"Submerged tenth!"

"Lethal chamber!"

—will do well to remind themselves that every class is sending, every day, nominations to swell the ranks down below, life is not all Bank Holiday for those born in the surroundings; it must be hell and brimstone for men who find themselves there, for the first time, in years of maturity.

Good nature is too precious to be wasted, and I am not going to ask that it should be squandered on the men who allow themselves to slide. They have some compensations. Everything else being equal, most folk would rather be excused from work, and whilst the industrious are rising early, rushing away to their duties, giving themselves the trouble and pain of striving, and encountering sometimes defeats, the drifter, during certain years has an easy time, lounging when others run, dawdling when others labour. If he has any sense he knows the penalties hitherto awarded to those whose behaviour he emulates, and he takes the risk. It is all a question of insurance. The average youth of town is aware that if he cares to devote evenings to hard study he can gain some special qualifications, and these will improve his chances in competition, later on, with his fellows; if he does not give his evenings to study, he may improve his handicap in billiards, he may become something of an authority, in a limited circle, on horses that race, but he knows that these abilities will not count for righteousness in Coleman Street. So that if the one demands congratulation on the arrival of success, the other must expect to be blamed when he reaches failure. The world is hard, but just. The chassé-croissé movement goes on; some go to the bottom, some go to the top. That is what happens here; what happens hereafter I do not for certain know. Failure in this life will surely not be looked upon as a valuable recommendation; I should be sorry, however, to think that only those who had achieved financial success were reckoned fit. You know the story of the millionaire who endowed hospitals, built churches and took all the precautions that money could arrange. He went out of life rather suddenly, and found—as he had expected to find—a handsomely appointed lift. The conductor asked whether he would mind waiting a while in case other passengers came; the millionaire, realising that now time no longer meant money, agreed. Becoming impatient a quarter of an hour later he gave a signal with finger and thumb.

"Conductor," he said, sharply, "what time is this lift supposed to go up?"

"It doesn't go up, sir," replied the conductor.

The world feels so incapable in regard to the men who have come down that its only plan is to give money to General Booth, ask him to do the best he can, and to express, privately, the hope that they may hear nothing more of the matter. In the shelters of the Salvation Army and in its labour-depots, I have found men of education and refinement, but of my own knowledge I have never found one of this type who showed any promise of recovery. It seems a journey for which return tickets are not issued. Once arrived at the last station, you remain there. There are no trains back. What I would like you to consider is, whether there is not some way of intercepting the traveller at a junction on the way, and of inducing him to change.

It is a junction where crowded trains meet, with passengers born in moderate circumstances who are making their difficult way up; with passengers born in excellent surroundings coming down on an easy gradient of one in twenty-five. Looking out, the men in the down trains must now and again be tempted to alight and to cross over, but the mere fact that they have come so far means they require the assistance of commanding, dogmatic maids. Sometimes, they surely perceive that they are acting the part of a fool; sometimes they must recognise that now or never exists their chance of making an alteration. At this junction then should assistance be given. I do not mean money is to be handed over; I do not ask that sympathy should be ladled out, but if they exhibit the least desire to turn, that desire ought to be encouraged. What they need, and what they have never had, is the process known as going through the mill; to the fortunate it comes in the early years. And the remedy for cases of the kind is twelve months hard labour.

I believe Homes of Industry for the mature would be a good investment for the country. The curse of idleness is much more serious than the curse of drink, and once a man had persuaded himself or had been persuaded to enter one 6i the Homes, his treatment would follow the lines applied to inebriates. The early days would have gentleness, and gradually and tactfully he would be encouraged to an active life. If he ever had any glimmering of talent, or of a trade, this would be fostered; a good deal of his life would be spent in the open air. Once into the swing of the movement, work and persistent work, work with scarcely a pause; work which sent him at night into a sound sleep that he had never known after lazy days. Attempts at malingering could be met and dealt with by the experienced, and a very definite course would be taken in regard to the miker. (I think the word is not to be found in the dictionary, and the derivation I cannot supply, but to mike is to do, by the exercise of ingenuity, less than your fellows.) In a case where the applicant had friends, it is conceivable that these would be willing to pay to the Home the sum they are now called upon to pay to shipping agents.

The great defect of the prison and the workhouse is, as that excellent man Mr Thomas Holmes has pointed out, that both teach an elaborate leisureliness, a trick of performing one hour's work in six, with the result that when the inmate comes out to a swift, busy world, he is unfitted to compete, unable to do anything more than make a feeble attempt to keep in step, one that he quickly relinquishes. In the Homes of Industry this error will not be committed. Men have been in the doctor's hands for the results of indolence; they rarely trouble him on account of over work, although it is one of the most precious joys to complain of excessive labour. The man who had done his twelve months might grumble, probably would grumble, but this the world could bear with equanimity; other people's complaints are not always catching.

It may be noted that the down trains stop at every station where there is a bar.

AT THE BAR

A friend of mine having written a serial story for a family magazine, one set of proofs, representing a month's instalment, was returned with a note pointing out, with regret, a serious indiscretion, and requesting it should be repaired forthwith. In a scene on board ship, two empty tumblers were referred to as being discovered on the captain's table; the editor recommended that coffee-cups should be substituted. This action represents a view considerable (without being broad), and whilst it is obvious to everybody that the roaring forties have gone, and that Mr Pickwick of to-day would probably be a teetotaller and a fruitarian, it may be that nervousness about making any printed reference to drink is aiding in the construction of a bogey in a fog; something which looms so threateningly that quiet folk run away from it. With many the word beer causes the eyelids to dose sharply; whisky—but this does not apply to Scotland or to Ireland—creates the convulsive shudder, the despairing groan. In spite of the title of the temperance movement, there are few subjects in regard to which it is so difficult to take a temperate view. At each end of the rope tremendous excitement is found, and presidents of Band of Hope societies use the forms adopted by leading articles in the Morning Advertiser; a large body of folk, interested in the tug of war, nevertheless make no shouting and scream no encouragement to either side because they have little sympathy with exaggeration, and because they are aware that the violence of one extreme is balanced by the fury of the other.

Reforms which have so far come in the drink habits of the people cannot be claimed by Parliament, although the King is generally made to promise something in the way of legislation, and the Houses do at times convert a Bill into an Act. I wish the results of an Act were always as good as its intentions. It is certain that when the Houses decided no child under fourteen should be served in a public house unless as a messenger conveying a sealed bottle, they honestly believed they were doing the wise, judicious thing. The actual consequences, so far as my observation goes, have been that, whereas in former days the youngster was dispatched with a jug and brought it back filled (taking slight toll on the way more as a declaration of independence than from any appetite for the beverage), now the mother or father has to take the jug, and being inside the cheerful public-house, feels that courtesy demands a drink should be ordered for consumption on the premises. If acquaintances are met there, the silly procedure of treating is perhaps started. Treating is, theoretically, a genial, hearty, hospitable system, but it works out disastrously in practice. In Paris, two men can go into a cafe, or into a zinc, have their drink together, and each will eventually settle for his own; here the etiquette is that drinks being paid for at the time of ordering, a struggle of politeness should take place, and when one party gives way, he does so with the remark,

"Well then, you must have a glass with me afterwards."

So that both, desiring but one glass and intending to take but one glass, find themselves compelled to take two. The best reform will come in when what is called Homburg fashion is introduced into the public bar.

Determined and dogmatic opinions in regard to the matter are expressed by those who sit in an easy-chair at their dub, with an electric bell-knob within reach. It does not appear to be realised by these that the average man also desires some of the comforts that a dub provides; a place where he can escape, for a time, home worries; can sit easily, discuss the behaviour of His Majesty's Ministers, listen to opinions of those in touch with borough councils, exchange chaff and stories. The average wife of the average man is not opposed to this hour of relaxation, and when the husband returns to supper—by which time the children are abed—she receives from him a bouquet of opinions culled from the world, a tribute at once to her intelligence and to his own observation. The evening papers can be seen in nearly every public-house, and if a customer should be disinclined for study, the proprietor or the ladies serving will furnish a brief precis of news of the day, with opinions and comments to guide the indefinite mind. The visit makes a holiday. The happiness of two domestic lives—I write as a bachelor—depends on correct abstention from each other's society; angels would quarrel if they did not make some excuse for occasional leave.

It may be regrettable on particular grounds that drink has intoxicating effects, but if this quality were absent, I really do not know how the hard-up folk would endure their existence. For us, when depression draws near, there are our friends with whom we can share it; there is the theatre, there are the railways imploring us by alluring advertisement to spend a week-end at Change-upon-Sea; by the side of the dashing young person who smiles from the poster, are the words, "Brilliant Sunshine, Unequalled Climate, Golf Links." The hard-up see this poster, but they have no interest in the prices quoted. The most convenient holiday open to them is one with a fare of twopence, and the distinct advantage of this excursion consists in the fact that—for a time—not only the surroundings are changed, but they themselves are altered. They acquire—for a time—a fluency of speech, they laugh at their troubles, they are prepared to forgive their enemies; sometimes, out of sheer good temper, they want to sing. True, they have to return from the holiday, and some depression ensues; but they have been away, and they can buoy themselves up with the prospect of, at some time in the future, going again. Strictly speaking, these are the only people who have a good excuse for drinking. I read the solemn remarks made occasionally by recorders and judges to grand juries, and I am willing to admit that I have known a few cases where appetite for drink has been the main cause of a man's failure in life. But against these few, one can place hundreds where the failure has come first, and the desire for drink has followed; and I am sure that there is nothing in me to justify, in these instances, the serving out of blame. Under similar circumstances, I should behave in an exactly similar manner.

The world, as it grows older, may discover other means by which the less fortunate can obtain temporary distraction. A risk endured by those who endeavour to peer into the future is that they assume life will always run on the existing lines; they make no allowance for new rails which may be laid down. I, at any rate, am not going to engage upon the task of speculation on 1958; I am more interested in the present year and in the people now living. If they find 1908 grey, it means little to them to be told that fifty years hence the days will be brighter. life is brief, and there is no necessity to encourage its cheerlessness. The public-house of today, generally conducted with care and reasonable wisdom, counts for brightness and, on the whole, for good humour; in the interests of moderate folk, especially in the interests of those to whom it furnishes something they cannot get elsewhere, I plead for its continued existence, and its theatre of the market penny.

THE MARKET PENNY

Mrs Parkson married about five years ago, and society in Deptford said of her at the time that she might have done better, and she might have done worse. Parkson was a good looking youth then, has a rather smart appearance in uniform now; he gives all this up on the Sundays when off duty, on which occasions he does a good deal of staying in bed, a little gardening, a considerable amount of smoking. He is the only man of my acquaintance who ever wears a dickey—a removable shirt front, popular in the country years ago—and this he assumes on the rare dates when he and the wife and their baby go to see his mother at Bermondsey. Mrs Parkson, when discussing personal and public affairs with the woman who shares with her the house in Gosterwood Street, often remarks that of course she knew he was but a railway porter at the time of the wedding, but she certainly had the impression that he would ascend the pay sheet—porter to guard, guard to inspector, inspector to station-master—and when news comes of some promotion, Parkson takes care to arrive home as late as possible. She was earning, before the marriage, nine shillings a week in a City warehouse, and the incident of her parcel of sandwiches being left in the train first threw them together,

"And I wish now" says Mrs Parkson, vehemently.

The favourite topic in these back garden debates is the remarkable good fortune of the un-wed female.

Yet she is fortunate. Parkson gains some extra money every day out of the thanks—offerings made by passengers, and this he keeps for his own uses. She does not know, and he is not precisely aware how much these sums come to in the course of a week; the comment is " Easy come, easy go." And to be quite fair, it can be admitted that Parkson serves himself adequately in regard to refreshment and tobacco, that his sixpence is always ready for any subscription set before him on pay-day, and that at the time when mysterious men strolled up and down near the cab-rank, accepting any slips of paper and coins presented furtively, he backed horses recommended to him by a parcel's cartman. Mrs Parkson's good fortune consists in the circumstance that the amount paid by the stationmaster's clerk on Thursday evenings is presented, whole and intact, to her. Sometimes she contends that, by rights, he ought to pay the three pence a week deducted for the sick fund, but against this her husband has several arguments, the most effective being a reference to the disastrous case of Mrs Shunter Davies.

Here then is Mrs Parkson with 17s. 9d. on each Thursday evening, and as her books are never submitted to a certified accountant, there exists some excuse for our impertinence in ascertaining how she disposes of the sum. Speaking generally, the details are as follows:—

	S. D.
Rent	5 6
Up-keep of boots, clothes, etc	1 6
Allowance to her mother	1 0
Coals, oil, etc.	1 6
Food, etc	8 3

Clearly this last item is not large; a good deal of wariness and acumen have to be exhibited in making about one and twopence a day serve the appetite of husband, wife, and baby. (I ought to mention that Parkson brings home the meat for Sunday's dinner, buying it out of his own extra money near Farringdon Street on Saturday nights.) How does she spend it? One is compelled to announce that she disburses the sum with deplorable prodigality. The recklessness that a Duke of Westminster might be pardoned for exercising is claimed by her. She pays about double value for everything, except milk. She does this, being all the time under the impression that she is a wonderful bargainer, that the folk are few and rare who get the best of her.

"You have to get up pretty early in the morning," she remarks acutely to shopkeepers' assistants in High Street, "to take me in!" The assistants give a jerk of the shoulders to intimate regret at discovering their limitations.

Take tea, for instance. Mrs Parkson takes tea, and buys it in lots of two ounces, which cost three pence. She does not expect, or desire, the best quality; she remains blind to the fact that she is getting the very worst, that she might almost as well use the dust on her mantelpiece. Bacon, again. Nothing is more acceptable or appetising than good rashers of bacon, but in purchasing one at the lowest price (a penny) she accepts an article that is but a chip of the old block on which it rests; fries it later in such a manner as to divest it of the last lingering suspicion of flavour. Vegetables. Mrs Parkson never had a good knowledge of the vegetable kingdom, and, by carefully assuming a knowledge, makes it certain she will never learn, so that Brussels sprouts fit only to be used as bullets are purchased by her; cauliflower rejected decisively by several customers and about to be written off by the greengrocer as a bad debt, is chosen and taken home in a sheet of the previous Sunday's paper, the news of which has a staleness that makes it an appropriate companion. Bread. Mrs Parkson cannot go far wrong in this regard, but she travels to the last terminus, and will buy anything that no one else desires. Beer. She might enrol herself amongst the strict teetotallers, for it is my belief she never has tasted beer in all the length of her life; instead she accepts in a jug the product that is a result, not of the hop garden, but of research on the part of chemists, and invention on the side of the publican.

Occasionally, the husband gives her a sum of money in order to add to the furnishing of the half house, and this, with unerring inaccuracy she lays out upon (say) a chair for five and nine that, launched from the Emporium near the Broadway with fair promise, becomes a complete wreck after a few weeks, unseaworthy and unlandworthy, so that chance visitors have to be warned not to trust themselves upon it. Her taste in vases for the sideboard is something of which one cannot speak calmly; her selection of linoleum appears to be based on an anxiety to get an article that will wear out; you require a pilot to get safely through the perilous passage at Gosterwood Street without accident. The rooms there are strewn with damaged goods. She took the baby—a little girl who has survived imperfect feeding—to a local photographer's (Cheapness is our Motto) a few months ago, and the picture has already faded. She has some idea of having it taken again, wants also to have herself taken before, as she says, all her good looks vanish, and there is no reason to suspect that she will avoid the previous error.

Thus you see Mrs Parkson, a youngish woman, referring to herself so often as a good manager, that she has come to believe in the truth of the description, a specimen of the female muddler, a fair sample of the squanderer. Proud of her strict economy, she is lavish; conceited in regard to her dexterity in handing out the market penny, she, to all intents and purposes, flings money away. It would be a mistake to assume that she will reform. It would be an equal blunder to think she wishes her child, when it grows up, to be any wiser than herself. She will probably resent any efforts made by the State to teach the girl the art of cooking, or laundry work, or domestic economy—"What's ben good enough for your mother is good enough for you!" And the State has to reckon sternly with the fatuous parent, and to make up its mind to show no sort of regard to arguments of the parrot cage, where new ideas are like the old.

THE YOUNG IDEA

There comes to every child brought up near to the lap of comparative opulence a moment when he has to face one difficulty; has to come to a decision, and make up his mind whether to keep up a pretence of believing in Santa Claus, and accept the December consequences, or to proclaim candidly fresh views. In the first method he is liable to the derision of contemporaries; in the second, he may earn a regretful sigh from parents.

It seems probable that the youngster brought up near to laps which cannot be called luxurious, will shortly be perplexed by a similar problem. He has written "Be Good and You will be Happy," with other lines of the same intent, and looked on as abstract propositions, he is not disposed to contest them; the fact, however, remains and exists on every side that those who are not good but slightly imperfect receive an attention and a kindness of a special nature, becoming the objects of such consideration that folk drop everything and run to watch. You have seen an expression in the eyes of demure horses on passing by a comrade who, having slipped on the asphalte, is engaging the interests of a crowd, with experts removing traces, backing the omnibus and making it easy for the recumbent animal to rise; you must have noticed on the part of the well-behaved horses something of reproof, but something, too, of envy.

The young men—and the young women—in the County Council schools feel that in ignoring the obvious, they are inviting the serious charge of childishness. For it is well known that a boy or girl of hard-up parents, or of parents lacking sense and the instincts of their position, is often, for some crime of a moderate nature—sleeping out at nights; taking a drink from milk-cans; snatching at a pair of boots—straightway mothered and fathered by the State, brought up in healthy conditions, becoming rosy-cheeked and sturdy, and so wisely instructed that at the age of sixteen, when the industrial schools bid farewell, it is well fitted to earn a living in the world. At a later date another object-lesson, much resembling the first, is presented.

An offender against the law of the land is now treated much as a dog who makes the earliest experiment in biting, and when it becomes necessary to inflict punishment then the generous machinery of what is known as the Juvenile Adult system sets to work; the young law-breaker finding himself at Wormwood Scrubbs in a cell not unlike the usual bed-sitting room of Kentish Town, with photographs of relatives on the wall, a supply of books that country houses do not always enjoy, whilst attractive opportunities are given for the learning of a trade, and energy is shown in obtaining for him, when he leaves, a good berth. In spare time he tills a flower bed, and in the evening excellent people lecture to him on Uganda.

What the old convicts on the other side think of all this, I am not aware, and if one knew one would probably be unable to repeat the comments. Remains the question of Press notices, a factor in our lives which all public men who subscribe to the useful agencies will understand; there arrives a satisfaction in this regard to be gained even by those whose desire it is to pursue their work secretly, whose rule it is to hide their light under a dark lantern. Once notoriety becomes forced upon them, they want plenty of it, and I am acquainted with a household in Dalston where cuttings from the columns headed "Police Intelligence" are preserved as family heirlooms; the proud mother knows them by heart. These are some of the compensations awarded to the adventurous; joys which the well-behaved rarely taste.

The great defect from which the average youngster suffers is that he is uninteresting. He is not of the stuff of which short stories are made. His atmosphere is not the atmosphere of romance. I believe that in spite of the better knowledge which has come in recent years of the missionary work necessary at home, funds can still be obtained for sending people out to distant countries to induce the residents there to exchange beliefs, and I am told that money can be most easily secured when the experiment is to be made on a body that is black or yellow. For the reason that the correctly-behaved child is white, it fails to gain attention; a smirch, and interest can immediately be shown.

Little need be said against the treatment accorded to the defective youngster, and, if anything could be said, it would not be said by me, but it seems worth while to point out that at present we are open to the charge of awarding special prizes for bad behavioiur. If I were a lad of twelve, living in (say) Shoreditch, I think I should be alert enough to recognise this, and should either make a spirited protest, or accommodate myself and my deportment to the circumstances. Collusion on the part of my parents; an air of truculence in the dock; a lecture from the magistrate, and my future would be assured. From that moment (as successful gentlemen say in interviews) I should never look back, but if at any time I happened to glance over my shoulder, it would be to smile at the efforts of well-behaved contemporaries.

The picture as it stands is out of drawing. I repeat that I don't want to see less consideration given at the reformatories, the industrial schools or at prisons, but I should like to see more encouragement given to those possessing a clear record. For the children who have absorbed knowledge, commendably and assiduously up to the age of, say thirteen, there should be centres to which it would be an honour to belong and a pleasure to attend. In the interests of bright particular climbers, a number of scholarships do exist, and they can go up the rungs of the educational ladder easily; I suppose they in their turn become teachers and assist in keeping the cycle moving.

My sympathies are—for a reason not difficult to see—with the mediocrities, who have done the best with the brains God has given them, but have no chance of reaching the giddy heights where instructors perch. To these, I would give a last year which should prepare them for some life other than—with the boys that of a messenger or van lad, and with the girl, other than that of cleaning steps. Considerable attention would be given in this year to their health, and amongst other things the boys might learn to play cricket (as the boys do at industrial schools) without losing temper. At present, the game as played in Regent's Park, for instance, resembles a political meeting where strangers have gained admission; the bowler cries " Out I " as he sends the ball down, and whether the ball hits the wickets or does not hit the wickets, whether the batsman is stumped or caught, or neither stumped nor caught, a delay occurs whilst everyone, at top of the voice.

screams an opinion. Incidentally, the last year might teach that when speaking to a colleague who stands at your elbow, it is unnecessary to adopt the tones of one training a crew on the river. More important would it be to ascertain from parents the career likely to be adopted by the child, and to give twelve months of wise and adroit preparation.

The inevitable consequences of doing things in the large lump are that one mould being used, only one shape is produced. A preparatory year would give opportunity for differentiation; it might also prevent the correctly-behaved child from envying the lot of one who, by a slide-slip, has contrived to engage the attentions of a stipendiary magistrate.

COMPARISONS IN HAPPINESS

There are so many views in regard to the situation of the impoverished of London, and their deportment, that no apology will be made for offering this contribution; as the applicant in the story said on being told by the foreman that there was only just enough work for the present hands, the little that I do is not likely to make much difference. If credentials are demanded, I am ready to answer that I have spent more than half of my life in watching the hard-up people of town, in making friends with them, and in writing about them; sometimes I seem to have succeeded in nothing but in achieving a very real and sincere affection for them. For the present purposes we will assume that I have discovered some of their secrets, and can reply to the question addressed by a recent post, "Are the people in the hard-up districts of town really happy or really unhappy?"

One can see the causes which have raised perplexity in the mind of the inquirer. She reads a book concerning these people wherein most of the characters are criminal, all the men brutish, the women, apes, lives made up of a series of violent assaults; speech consisting of imprecations; the one and only god, beer. To many, this kind of fiction is extremely comforting, enabling them to regard the unsuccessful as they would gaze at caged animals in the Zoological Gardens, and feeling thankful sufficient protection exists between themselves and the objects. Moreover, this view encourages the smug assurance that nothing can be done for those down in the basement of society, and that any efforts to make experiments in this direction are certain to achieve nothing but failure; the cheque book accordingly continues to send its slips to the secretaries of those Missionary Societies which undertake to prove that black can be made white. Also, this kind of book shocks the average mind, and one of the greatest errors we can make is to assume that the average mind dislikes to be shocked. It is when the anxious reader comes across another volume giving an account of folk in the position of life occupied by those in the first book and describing them as living lives odd but not offensively eccentric, crediting them with good humour, a genuine regard for each other, and a determination to make the best of their surroundings, with here and there ambition and extraordinary pluck—then it is the student who has not personal knowledge of the characters and has to rely, for information, on the printed word, finds the mind perturbed, and becoming seriously concerned, wails aloud the inquiry to which Pontius Pilate obtained no answer. I suggest, with deference, that those in search of truth had better depend on the second book than on the first. In the course of my wanderings and my investigations I have met nearly all the types, from murderers in Rotherhithe to nurses at Medical Missions, and I declare I have found little to justify the congregation of monsters described in certain works of fiction. They have the faint resemblance to originals to be detected in the caricatures by Mr Max Beerbohm; one can admit that sometimes they are presented with like cleverness. Those who take their pictures from these artists must wonder why, with the Thames so near and so broad and so deep, the folk depicted should continue to live; by all the rules Bethnal Green, if it were the Bethnal Green of these books, would surely march through Bishopsgate and Gracechurch Street, and, reaching London Bridge, put an end to its intolerable existence in the waters below. You are requested to observe that, as a fact, it is not Bethnal Green, but gentlemen residing in the Temple and ladies of South Kensington who take up the hobby of suicide. Bethnal Green may occasionally take the life of another person; it counts its own too precious for unhappy dispatch. Without attempting to give a perfect definition of the word happiness, one may suggest it is a quality which cannot be claimed by any one bored with his own existence, tired of himself, and this is a condition you rarely find in the hard-up districts of London. Added, there exists the feeling of resignation (I do not count this amongst their virtues; one would rather see them dissatisfied and resentful) which enables them to accept the cuts and blows with a sigh and the remark, "Ah well, I s'pose it had to be!" The man in the Temple with one imperfect tooth in an otherwise excellent set, raves and storms, protesting against the vengeful attitude of Providence, calling the world to witness that he has done nothing to deserve this cruel treatment; there was once an old lady in East Street, Walworth, who confided to me that she had only two remaining teeth in her head, "But, thank 'eaven," she said piously, "thank 'eaven, they're both opposite each other!"

Those of us, eager to see the next generation in the minor neighbourhoods of town, better than the present, gain nothing by extravagance of statement, and it can be declared at once that the hard-ups, taken in the lump, are by no means unhappy. I may agree they ought to be unhappy; that is another matter. A considerable amount of their cheerfulness is due to the fact that their lives possess the element of a gamble, and extraordinary things, which to us would appear ordinary, may happen at any moment. A boy in Somers Town who earns a halfpenny, or finds one, knows the exultation that comes to a Chairman of a limited company (in which he holds most of the shares), when announcing a dividend of fifteen per cent.; the woman of Kensal Rise who obtains a new and excellent customer for her laundry shares the satisfaction of one making a curtsey at Buckingham Palace. It is all a matter of proportion, and our own sums are never the sums of other people. Thus the hard-up folk reckon a kindness shown to them much beyond its value as seen by the giver, although in London they are generally not shy enough to express their feelings, and a boy trembles with delight when he wins a shilling knife at boxing; a girl becomes scarlet when she is presented, for ability in some other direction, with a sixpenny book. These things have to be remembered in making an estimate of happiness. The very rareness of their amusements enables these folk to esteem highly the amusements which come their way. To the youngsters, a horse down in the street is a performance at the Hippodrome; a bemused individual on his way home is a comedy at the Criterion, an argument between man and wife is a lively debate in the House of Commons. To the grown-ups, the behaviour of Mrs Somebody next door but one is what the publishers call a piquante society novel; acquisition of a new pair of vases at the sixpence halfpenny shop in Upper Street the furnishing of a new town house; a trip to Southend on the August Bank holiday a voyage to Australia and back.

Perhaps it would be well to call some witnesses, and that I may not overstate the case, I will issue a subpoena—they are not likely to attend willingly—to the members of two families of my acquaintance who have much in common with each other, and we will take first the Clanks in Somers Town. The provincial reporter in describing village concerts generally has the sentence "Where many are so good, it becomes invidious to particularise," and with a slight alteration one might use the phrase. I have not been able to discover a family entirely bad; just as in most households in another sphere there is generally one disastrous sheep, so in Somers Town it would puzzle you to find a tenement dwelling where something good did not exist. Such groups could be invented, but, for the moment, I am not writing fiction. I am going to introduce to you the Clanks of Little Clarendon Street, N.W., London born and London bred. The immigrant alien has not yet reached Somers Town; when he does arrive there it will probably be found that figures of crime decrease, and that ambition becomes more apparent. The Clank family should be interesting; interesting in any case, to the rate-payers, since the education of their children has cost the country, I find, a lump sum of £156; the parents just escaped the Act of '70, and this accounts for a good deal. I know them well, for they live within a stone's throw of my rooms, a fact which ought to imperil my windows; they will certainly give me no thanks for telling you of them, since they are almost alone in not wanting to be talked about; their general custom being to do harm by stealth and blush to find it fame. The Clank family consists of Mr and Mrs Clank—father and mother—three boys and two girls; there were two other baby girls, and dates of the funerals of these can be fixed by Mrs Clank (a great believer in the insurance of children's lives) because, on each occasion, the police came down little Clarendon Street in couples at about midnight. Mrs Clank makes the beds every evening at ten o'clock, and she does her washing on Saturdays. The washing hangs out upon the railings in a singularly frank and open way, and the appearance of the articles is so little changed by the process that it would seem to be more a form of ritual than anything else; their value may be guessed from the fact not one garment is ever lost.

Clank has the air of one with whom misfortune has walked hand-in-hand; this perhaps is why he grumbles half-aloud as he strolls alone in Somers Town. By profession, a house painter, the last work of art on which he was engaged cannot be exhibited, for the ravages of time have affected it, necessitating application of two or three coats from another brush. Meanwhile, Clank is a snapper up of unconsidered trifles in the way of odd jobs, sometimes moving a family on a borrowed truck, sometimes helping in a mews, sometimes demanding work from the parish (and this being furnished, performing it with great sulkiness and every sign of incapacity) sometimes a servile attendant at a cab-rank.

He finds a considerable grievance in the fact that his health remains good, for if it were otherwise, pity and help would be extended to him, London would hurry to his assistance, and make much of him; he will tell you that throughout the whole course of his existence he has never had what he calls a fair chance. Like many unsuccessful men, he believes in luck. He has frequently announced this in the public bar of "The Seymour Arms." The family scoff at most authorities and carry on war against most representatives of capital, but they have a profound admiration and regard for the proprietor of "The Seymour Arms." The publican makes a link between themselves and respectability and order; a man friendly in a reserved, dignified way with them» who has nevertheless been seen to enter a police court and shake hands with an inspector.

Members of the Clank family sometimes go to a London police court; James, the eldest son, goes often enough to be able to discriminate better than most of us between the parties compelled to attend there.

The court makes a place of public entertainment for those who have discovered how grateful it is to contemplate the troubles of other people. Here are applications, before the hearing of cases, with a succession of men and women at the witness-box, each obsessed by a grievance, each trembling with righteousness, some endeavouring to engage the sympathies of the magistrate by calling him "My Lord," or "Your Grace."

And this over, one morning, some years ago, the sergeant announced,

"Number fifteen, your worship, James Clank!"

James, eldest son of the Clank family, smooths his splosh of hair over his forehead, and, on first introduction to a magistrate, prepares to fight considerable odds. The proprietor of the boot shop, unwilling to waste time over small matters, has sent an assistant to give the necessary evidence, and when he has furnished this, the magistrate's clerk puts one or two questions. Is he certain the boots produced are the property of his firm? Yes. How does he identify them?

By marks. By what marks? The assistant turning the articles over fails (for a reason known to James) to discover the signs, and presently says so. James Clank, swift to detect the changes of fate, leans forward and of the magistrate begs permission to ask a question: the magistrate assures him his interests are safe and himself takes the witness in hand. The witness has said that before the boots were missed, he saw James loafing about in front of the shop in Hampstead Road; is the witness certain of the identity of James? Let witness think and consider before answering. Witness, damp with nervousness, seems now disinclined to believe in the identity of anything, and replies cautiously that James resembles the man. This won't do at all. The magistrate feels it necessary to warn the witness. Can he or can he not say that—? No, to be quite candid, witness cannot say.

Very well then, it comes to this; witness cannot identify the boots, cannot identify the man. That, admits the witness penitently, is about the size of it. The magistrate with a crowded charge list to deal with, dips pen in ink, discharges the prisoner; James goes out of the door near to where the public stand, and the folk there give a murmur of congratulation; the boots are returned to him and in accepting them and looking to see whether by chance the size is his, he endeavours to assume a wronged air. The contest of James Clank versus Law and Order stands at that moment one love.

I am inclined to think the contest would go on even though James lost the first game; it certainly continues under the encouraging circumstances. James is of the type that cannot distinguish kindness from weakness, fairness from semi-idiocy. I meet James later at Borstal prison near Rochester where, on a well-proved charge of burglary, he is serving two years. Being below the age of twenty-three he is treated under the admirable new system, wearing a demure uniform, allowed to work with others in the garden, to converse with them, to learn by day a trade if he be so minded; in the evening the chaplain plays chess with him and loses. The governor in showing me round calls James, and James comes up, respectful, answering questions alertly. Yes, James feels very comfortable at Borstal, and has no word to say against the officials. When James leaves, he will leave with regret, tempered by the fact that the authorities will do their best to obtain for him a situation, and enable him to take up, as a novelty, an honest life. James has had enough of trouble, and assures the governor, assures me, that he intends never again to enter into battle with Law and Justice. This would be excellent and good and satisfactory, and I know the generous treatment often works well, but a wink that James gives me so soon as the governor's back is turned suggests he has views in reserve which, for diplomatic reasons, he does not give to the Governor of Borstal. He costs the State £17 a year, and I fear the State will on many future occasions entertain him as an unwilling and a nonpaying guest.

Henry William, second son of the Clank family, I think you may know, at least you must have seen him. He is often outside Euston Station; he would be inside only that many of the North Western officials have prejudices, and large, strong hands. Never one of your slaves to fashion, following its whims and fancies, he wears a straw hat all the year round, for which reason his friends call him Maizypop, and this name has been adopted so generally that the other day at an inquest, it took him some time to remember his real surname and furnish it to the Coroner, There was more trouble later in the afternoon, because the Coroner suggested Maizypop might have jumped into the canal and saved the child's life, but as Maizypop pointed out, to have done this would have looked like interference, and might have resulted in a nasty cold. His motto is "Mind your own business," and the fact that he has no business of his own makes it impossible to say whether or not he would himself practice the teaching of the motto. One can have opinions on the subject.

Maizypop, this second son of the Clank family, belongs to the class in Somers Town known as born-tireds. He does nothing, he says little, his nightmare is work. I have spent hours and days and months in the endeavour to find out how he and his similars manage to live, and to be quite frank, no sort of success has attended my efforts. I know they do live, that they eat and they drink and they smoke, but where and how they obtain the money—they cannot be always borrowing from each other—I am unable to say and Maizypop will not tell me. He remarks vaguely that he manages to pick up a bit, that he contrives to rub along, but this does not explain. What I want is to be allowed to inspect his books, to look through his accounts. Maizypop is able to enjoy London, or that small part of it which he knows; he is not underfed and he is always talking about backing horses. He is parochially-minded, with a district bounded on the north by Camden Road, the south by Euston Road, on the east by Pancras Road, on the west by Albany Street; if he found himself outside of this neighbourhood he might have to appeal to a constable, which would make him feel shy. He has never been in trouble—this on account of sheer laziness—but his grievance against the S. division is that they can never leave a chap alone to the enjoyment of rest. Will keep him on the move! He is harried to such an extent by the S. division, that he declares sometimes he scarce dares to call his soul his own; I feel tolerably certain that no one else would care to claim it.

There remains, of the male members of the family, the boy Cyril. Cyril is young and he has possibilities; at present I see him the shuttlecock in a game played on one side by the State, on the other side by his own deplorable family. During the hours of nine till twelve of the morning, and two till half-past four of the afternoon in five days of the week, the State appears to be winning hands down; Cyril in school is a fairly well-behaved lad, obedient to his teachers, learning the precise chronological order of kings and queens, able to recite the principal exports of Java, and, in regard to his eleven times, a great deal nearer accuracy than I myself can arrive. His boots are imperfect, and he wears no jacket or collar; if clothes are presented to him by a friend of the headmaster at the Aldenham Street County Council schools, they disappear as though made the subject of a conjuring trick. Really, Cyril is more comfortable without them, for life is hard in Somers Town for a boy with a new garment; an inconvenient superstition inducing other boys to pinch the wearer.

Cyril sings before school finishes for the day the doxology with great enthusiasm and marches out, a well-drilled, demure boy through the playground. Once clear of the iron gates, once outside the walls of the playground, he suddenly throws off the bonds of propriety and order; becomes, on the instant, a shrieking, tearing, screaming youth, rushing here and there like a mad dog, quarrelling with his fellows, snatching off their caps and using them for a game of football, upsetting the contents of barrows in Ossulston Street, ringing bells at private houses, and behaving generally as one who has never endured method, never come under control. I, myself, should not care to claim entire responsibility for Cyril, but if I may say so with conceit, I can manage him for a couple of hours occasionally. He comes to the schools on an evening once in a fortnight, and he elects to come into my room to practice the art of boxing. When he first came, he filled in the time of waiting for the gloves by noisily deriding the efforts of others, by leading the tempestuous spirits in ribald remarks. Then I hit upon an idea so good, that I think I must have borrowed it from some one. "Clank, old chap," I said, "I want you to do me a favour. You're the only man in this room I feel I can trust. I want you. Clank, to be master of the ceremonies. When you are not boxing, keep the other boys in order. If they don't obey you, report them to me."

Young Cyril Clank, before that, rebel and mutineer, is now such a martinet, such a stern preserver of absolute silence, that one sometimes has to beg of him to temper Justice with Mercy, lest the boxing-room should become a Siberian Penal Settlement. We are going to try to obtain a berth for him when he leaves school, and I believe that if he gets into a suit with brass buttons, all may go well. Uniform treatment will perhaps make a man of him. Meanwhile my sympathies are all on the side of the State and against the influences of home, and I wish that "Time!" had not to be called when the boy reached the age of fourteen.

There remain of the Clank family, two daughters. Good to report that neither is living in Little Clarendon Street. The elder, called Lizzie, came before the magistrate—you would not remember the case in the newspapers, there are so many of the kind—charged with the serious offence of being out of her parent's control, and Lizzie's mother in the witness-box on that occasion was a model of behaviour for all hardly tried parents for all time. Mrs Clank, tears in eyes, avowing a preference for a serpent's tooth, assured the magistrate that she had done everything possible to mortal woman in looking after the child, had been kind to her, had been severe with her, had been more like a friend than a mother, but somehow Lizzie preferred sleeping in a four-wheeled cab that rested for the night in a mews near King's Cross to the ease, comfort, luxury of Little Clarendon Street.

Lizzie, away in the country, kept and fed by the State at a cost of £35 a year and being trained to become a decent member of society, likes her new parents better than the old—see the ingratitude of children!—and in Little Clarendon Street she is held to have disgraced herself and become unworthy of being reckoned a member of the family. I think they would be inclined to disinherit her and to cut her off with a shilling, but to do this would not only be treatment more generous than that previously extended to any member of the family; it would also interfere with great expectations. For what Mr and Mrs Clank hope is that so soon as a situation is found by the State for the accomplished Lizzie, she will contribute a good amount of her earnings towards the up-keep of the good old home.

"After all," argues Mrs Clank, "blood ought to count. Even Daisy recognises that."

Daisy, the younger girl, aged fourteen and a half, is engaged as general servant in a lodging-house in Harrington Square, at £8 a year. At the age of ten Daisy began to work in spare moments, going round on Saturdays clothed in a way that suggested a game of jumping in sacks, and, giving a single knock at doors, offered assistance. It may be truly said of her that she proceeded step by step, for now and again some matron, impressed by the excellent results achieved by Daisy at the front of the house, provided tasks of a more exalted character within, investing her with the title of Odd Girl. They found her willing (which in view of all the circumstances was amazing enough), they discovered she was honest (and this, in view of the same circumstances, was in explicable). Daisy soon found that if she took all the money she earned to Little Clarendon Street, her mother denounced her violently for retaining some for her own uses, and the girl decided to adopt the suggestion, making of one of the matrons her banker, and placing on Saturdays as much as fourpence on deposit account. She left school one Friday afternoon for good, and the same evening—the very same evening—went into service. Daisy is a wonderful little woman; there seems no accounting for her. Most of us are no better than we ought to be; Daisy forms an exception.

What is her day? Well, she rises at half-past six, having been up twice in the short night, once because young Ethel thought she had a touch of earache and awoke to discuss the question; once when young Bert found himself violently seized, and bound to the stake by a number of Red Indians, and a lighted torch about to be applied to the faggots. She dresses the landlady's youngsters, declaring this a task they should be capable of performing for themselves; she herself did it at the age of three and a half. On the way downstairs she collects boots and shoes from outside doors, and in the kitchen throws these into a comer, expressing regret that some people can never learn how to walk without picking up all the mud. She lights the fire, and the cat strolls in. Daisy upbraids the cat and demands to be informed where it has been all night, inventing answers in such an apologetic tone that the cat assumes a mournful and a penitent attitude, from which it emerges, when the bang and chink and clatter come of the milkman's cart. A pleasant interlude here for Daisy. Convention demands of the milkman, when she has imbarred the area door, that he should ask whether she is prepared to come along with him to St James's Church; convention prescribes that Daisy should answer that so long as her eyesight remains good, she will never be attracted by the milkman. Convention requires that the milkman should thereupon threaten to put an end to his life in the Regent's Canal, and convention orders that Daisy should reply, looking into the can of milk which he has handed to her, that he appears to have been there already. With this libel on his wares, the brief flirtation closes.

She makes two cups of tea and takes them to the door of the landlady's room. Her name is shouted from the floors above with a demand for hot water.

"And now I've got to bustle!" says Daisy.

Daisy is upstairs and downstairs, making beds in one place, scrubbing the linoleum in the other, never still for a moment, and pursued by her mistresses voice wherever she may be.

"Are you upstairs, Daisy? Then come down, this minute."

"Are you downstairs, Daisy? Then come up, and don't let me have to bawl at you."

Through the fierce shower and hailstorm of demarcation, Daisy works steadily on, beginning presently to look forward to one o'clock and dinner. The two children come home at ten minutes past twelve, full of some important event that has happened at school, and desirous to have a game of horses with Daisy in the back garden, themselves taking the part of coachmen. She sits down with the family for the mid-day meal and here she is well treated.

"Let me see!" says her mistress, "you like the well done, don't you?"

Work again, so soon as the children are kissed and sent away, and a good hard determined afternoon it is, I promise you. A room to turn out, heavy articles of furniture to be lifted; windows at a perilous height to be cleaned and, after a rest and a wash and change of dress and cap, serious preparation for dinner for those young men who require an evening meal. At the end of the day, at half-past eleven, Daisy takes her candle and goes upstairs, and she generally says to herself that she will succeed in going to sleep without rocking.

Thursday evening is the time of which she speaks with fond and gleeful anticipation, and if one of the lodgers rallies her about anxiety to meet her young man, she does not deny the soft imputation. I know it is quite wrong, and you know it is perfectly reprehensible that Daisy—not fifteen yet—should act in this way, but we will not grudge her the small romance.

life is for her a book printed in such large capitals that the wonder is she has any illusions left; it helps very much in her strenuous duties day after day to be able to think that somewhere there is—not a prince on a white charger, not a member of the House of Lords pretending to be an artist, but a good, honest, clean journeyman carpenter—and that somewhere, and somewhen, she will meet him. At the Camden Theatre, three minutes away, on the Thursday evening, she, giving a keen glance around, runs along the high pavement of Crowndale Road, turns down Charrington Street, doubles back and stops at the entrance of Little Clarendon Street to regain breath, and to avoid stepping on babies. Daisy's arrival is an event sufficiently important to give excuse for the relinquishment of the perfunctory attention to domestic duties. Matrons come out and swear casually at their offspring fighting in the roadway, and comment audibly, satirically, on Daisy's appearance.

"Some of us fancy ourselves, don't we? What a difference another person's hat does make, to be sure!"

"Fine feathers make fine birds, but they don't fetch no more at the poultry shop."

"Won't look so perky when she comes out. Stiff-starched and double-blued now, but just wait until her mother's had a talk to her. She won't stand any of her nonsense."

"If the girl follows her nose, she ought to go to heaven!"

To tell the truth Mrs Clank has made some endeavour to prepare for the visit of her younger daughter; the deal coalbox has been placed on the worst space of the carpet, the table has been scrubbed, and Mrs Clank has taken the extraordinary step of rolling down her sleeves and wetting her hair with the palms of hands. Mrs Clank nods as Daisy enters, gives a sniff of self-compassion, and is about to ask, in whining tones, whether the girl has brought anything, when Daisy goes to the window and pushes it up. It comes down again at once, and the girl places a bundle of firewood to keep it in position.

"Fresh what?" echoes Mrs Clank, in a scream.

"Fresh air," repeats Daisy, composedly.

"You get some nice silly notions into that 'ead of yours," remarks her mother, with vehemence. "You're getting spoilt, that's what's happening to you. Leave off fidgeting about, do, and set down and let me talk to you."

Mrs Clank has a good deal to say, the accumulated news of the week has to be given, and she becomes so much absorbed in the task that she fails to notice Daisy (who cannot be idle), is putting the room straight, blowing dust from the mantelpiece, making up the fire and filling the kettle.

Presently Mrs Clank breaks off to express an opinion.

Always on the same rock disaster occurs! Daisy's solid and unbending argument is that beer is not good for her mother; Mrs Clank's contention is that beer is sent into this world, and to refrain from drinking as much as you can get. Is to behave with impiety; she has a lurking suspicion that there is something in the Bible to confirm this view. The condensed milk foimd and sugar borrowed, Mrs Clank admits she has tasted, in her time, a worse cup, and the neighbour who lent the sugar is invited to share the beverage. Others come to the doorway in the hope of receiving a similar invitation, and the fact that a selection of these is made, gives rise to one of those quarrels which mark and distinguish Little Clarendon Street. A quarrel of words at first, Daisy endeavouring to interfere diplomatically, assuring the contending parties that each is in the right and each in the wrong. Mrs Clank rolls back sleeves and announces with relish that she is going to set about one or two of them; an eager crowd gathers at the door, begging that the fight may take place in the street where all can see fair and if necessary join. At the first blow, Daisy, knowing that she can do nothing to arrest the inevitable, runs, shamefaced through Little Clarendon Street, runs until she can again breathe the fresh air of decency, glad to find herself again in Harrington Square, content to hear the nagging voice of her mistress, and willing to go up to her room and have a good cry.

Turn from the Clank family in Little Clarendon Street, and glance at the Yorke-Bullens in West Kensington.

The Yorke-Bullens are well-connected, and this circumstance will be intimated to you ere you have been listening to any member of the family for two minutes; there exists one political relative, who, when in office, was referred to as a first cousin; the relations became more distant when he lost his seat at the last election. The father has an annuity, one which has been regularly paid by a business-like Government for some years, the mother has money of her own; the son, always referred to as poor Wally, is away in Montreal, the three daughters live at home. The mother, an amiable soul, not presuming to dictate to her children on many points, showed years ago tremendous determination and unbending obstinacy in regard to their acquaintances and friends, and one of the rules most completely impressed upon the daughters was that they must keep to their' own class, never travelling in a compartment inferior to that for which they hold a ticket; they must in short not associate with passengers travelling third. The Yorke-Bullen girls—now at an age when they are content to be referred to as girls, and sometimes, for encouragement of this, assuming many of the tricks of juvenility—in consequence find themselves not rarely without companions, without engagements, without occupation, without callers, and the youngest includes amongst her duties the task of giving an air of modernity to contents of the card-tray, which she effects with the aid of a piece of india rubber. The family would be shocked and indignant at the suggestion, but the members have many tricks in common with the Clanks of Somers Town. The father—I like the old chap, but I cannot persuade many men to give their minds to his conversation— can generally be relied upon to start at breakfast some topic which at once introduces civil war into the family, and the day starts under these auspices. They separate, after the meal, on the worst possible terms and he reads his newspaper, of which he will lend not so much as the fashion page, will share not a printed word until he has, in his deliberate way, made himself, to some extent, master of the news, slave of the leading article. Later, he invites the attention of his wife, who has to sit, doing some fancy work adapted for use only in the regions of fancy, whilst he serves out to her sparingly items of information selected from the journal, accompanying them with eloquent criticisms, couched in language that would shock Little Clarendon Street where the number of adjectives is strictly limited to three; if public men sometimes find themselves trembling suddenly or afflicted for no reason obvious to them, with an attack of fright, I am m a position to explain the cause. His wife agrees cautiously.

"I suppose there's a good deal in what you say, Henry!"

Or,

"But don't you think that perhaps they are trying their best?"

Or the safer remark of,

"Ah well, it will be all the same to us a hundred years hence!"

Mr Yorke-Bullen takes the Underground at noon to St James's Park Station, and the walk across the park constitutes the most violent exercise he allows himself; brags of this ten minutes' promenade in the dub until it becomes, to his mind, a feat having resemblance to the climbing of the Himalayas. He grumbles about the excellent lunch provided at a reasonable price, declaring the race of good chefs has become extinct; the best cooking existed at the time when he was aged between twenty and thirty. All the same, he over-eats himself and in the smoking-room, the waiter there has to watch the cigar and place it in a position where it can bum safely whilst Mr Yorke-Bullen sleeps. He awakes in an atrocious temper, ready to quarrel with any member of like state of mind, and, this over, makes the announcement that he is now about to dear up his correspondence, for which task fresh nibs have to be brought, the blotting-paper renewed and the date furnished to him seven times. He squares elbows and sets to work. You will find the stationery rack filled later with the initial efforts of a "My dear sir" and a blot, or "To the Editor," and a few thoughtful scratches, or "My dearest Wally" and a rough drawing, done apparently whilst thinking of other subjects, of the map of Canada. Eventually, he rings for the waiter and informs him of a decision to postpone the writing of letters until to-morrow—"Be sure to remind me, George!" the waiter answers "Yes sir, certainly sir!"—and Mr Yorke-Bullen goes down the steps of the club with the air of a man who has done a day's good work.

He does not take tea, but his daughters have a thirst for the beverage not easily quenched, and they have used the hours from four till half-past five in making calls at flats where hostesses show in receiving them enthusiasm and vivacity, which diminish as the Yorke-Bullen girls talk. Themselves under the impression that they are brilliant conversationalists, it is not always possible to force people to take this view, and impartial judges would be likely to agree with the hostesses. The girls have the ability of dealing with any subject and at once rendering it without interest. They can make a mole-hill out of a mountain. It would be a troublesome matter to convey on paper an idea of the conversational methods of the Misses Yorke-Bullen on occasions when they produce their best behaviour; the vacuity of it, the fatuousness of the arguments, the blank emptiness of the views; the leading rule appears to be that they must never say exactly what they think. This is why sometimes you will see their eyes water when they talk; they are stifling a yawn for which there exists a good and satisfactory excuse. When the hostess says, rising, "Well this has been a short visit," they accept the hint and, before going, speak in tones of complaint of the demands upon their time, managing to convey the flattering suggestion that calling on friends and taking a. cup of tea is one of the duties against which they particularly rebel. At dinner at home—the girls are rarely asked out to this meal, because it proves a delicate matter to select one, and to invite three is admittedly out of the question—at dinner in the home they make add references to folk they have met; the father recites a slightly improved version of an argument he has had; the mother says it is a queer world. If by chance the girls go to a theatre, they depart with the emphatic prophecy, based seemingly on a knowledge of themselves, that they feel certain they are not going to enjoy the play. When staying in they fill the time by pointing out to each other family faults, conspicuous or partially hidden.

Apart from the question of courtesy, one has adequate personal reasons for not wanting to talk of dates, and I am only going to say I have known them for many years and that the eldest once—an awkward side slip, not likely to happen now—once referred to the views she took as a child, when she heard of the death of the Prince Imperial; the youngest takes pains to give information privately that a considerable interval exists between herself and the other two. I can remember the time when they permitted their features to take an air of interest when occasion gave excuse, but those days are past and having assumed a look of general distaste for the world under the idea that this conferred upon them a manner of superiority, they now succeed in making the attitude fit the expression. Their voices have a complaining note, and when disputing with each other, they use a considerable number of phrases intended to hurt and exasperate; the mother, called in when sore throat begins to supervene, declares she finds a striking resemblance to the parrot-house at the Zoological Gardens.

In point of fact the three girls quarrel just as much as any three women in Little Clarendon Street, and their wordy contests are more prolonged because, with them, there can be no decision by an appeal to arms and fists. The mother, varying her simile, occasionally asserts the three live a cat and dog life, but this is an unfair comparison which no lover of animals would apply; there seems more of reasonableness in the comment that she wishes to goodness one or all would become engaged and eventually married and set up homes of their own. Time, says the mother, does not stand still; they are growing older every day, and people are beginning to talk. These phrases scarcely represent tact in its highest form, and they goad the family into making retorts which bring a ready tear to the mother's eye. To be quite fair, there is much to be said in excuse for the girls' failure. The only profession to which they have been brought up is that which consists in securing a husband, and the shallowest young man of their acquaintance knows this as well as they and their mother know it, and he knows too that they think he does not know it. Young women in the Savings Bank Offices near Addison Road, are often ridiculed by the Misses Yorke-Bullen; their hats described satirically, their manner of hurrying to and fro, reproved, but—assuming marriage to be the desire of most women—these girls in a Government department, with their good salaries and their busy, well-furnished lives are in point of fact much more attractive to the average male than the Yorke-Bullens. The wage-earning girl is obviously independent, she shews no haste to get married, her days are full and she has not to scheme and plan to make them occupied; all this combines to make a presentation of casual indifference which, believe me, engages the attention of youth and makes youth determined to conquer. Moreover, in spite or because of their position in society, the Yorke-Bullens, supposing they were able to choose, have not the same choice that is offered to the Savings Bank girl; they certainly do not share the opportunities of increasing the circle of acquaintances that will come, for instance, to Daisy Clank.

Small wonder then that the outlook becomes, every day, more like the contents of a cruet-stand; if the girls cannot say anything of a vinegar nature, they prefer to remain silent. They have never assisted in the kitchen, of which fact they brag as though it were something deserving the Order of Merit; they can, in moments of stress and urgency, sew in a way that permits the stitches to unravel without difficulty; they paint just well enough to enable them to give their works as wedding presents to folk for whom they do not care, and to justify them in holding strong views concerning the Royal Academy. They have never yet brushed a boot, or swept a floor. They read a good deal, and it is one of their boasts that they cannot remember the title of a book or the name of an author, or the nature of a plot, when five minutes have elapsed after finishing the last page; their criticisms are two in number and brief; either a book is "absolutely delightful," or it is "unspeakable." They play the pianoforte, and the youngest has some grim thought of taking up the violin, this mainly because her father declares the sound of the fiddle detrimental to his nerves. The middle girl tells folk she has half a mind to go in for Christian Science and begs them earnestly to tell her exactly what they think about it, but when they attempt to do so, allows her attention to take a stroll about the room. Believing themselves models of good manners, and exceedingly critical in regard to the manners of other people, they are obviously unaware the veneer is so thin that most lookers-on can see through it; I declare I prefer the deal table of Somers Town to the mahogany of West Kensington. Finally, to offer the last piece of information concerning the family, they never give away a penny unless under exercise of main force and violence on the part of their vicar, and Yorke-Bullen, the father, has often described to me a great scheme of his, whereby all men and women who have not sufficient to live upon would be conducted, by the police to a lethal chamber.

Compare the lives of these two families, consider the money advantages possessed by one over the other, give due allowance for the differences in aspirations and then stand back and make your decision. Make the decision for yourself. For my own part, I am of opinion that the Clanks, a deplorable family enough, get more happiness out of life than the Yorke-Bullens, and, in all fairness, if there is pity to be given away, one ought to extend sympathy to West Kensington rather than to Somers Town. Let me add an important rider. In Little Clarendon Street are young people who feel rebellious at their surroundings, who want to get out of the cage, who know there are better and brighter lives to be lived. And in looking on the grown-up Clanks with Conservative equanimity, one can, at the same time, be more socialistic than any socialist where the children are concerned.

The first step is to make them clean, and help them to keep clean.

NEIGHBOUR TO GODLINESS

The most obvious triumphs achieved by the County Council schools have been in the direction of decorum, and in the removal of a popular prejudice against soap and water. I am old enough to remember the time when a clean-faced child in certain London streets was derided for that, and for no other reason ("'Ere's the kid who washes twice a day!" declared the amused critics). It was but the other afternoon I encountered in Islington a kind of Vigilance Committee, of which no member exceeded ten years of age, a committee that was reprimanding a child in emphatic language which left no room for misapprehension, for the breach in good manners in touching another boy's hoop with hands which even a sycophant could not have called white. Some years ago at a school in Walworth two small girls were sent to the wash-hand basin, and there as they shared a towel, one said with pride,

"My face was a lot grubbier than what yours was!"

"Yes," admitted the other, "but you're older!"

At the very moment of writing, a long string of youngsters marches below my window carrying small linen-bags, with a governess in command; the children are on the way to the baths to take exercise in swimming, and will presently return with hair rather straight, but normal good temper and vivacity considerably improved. I submit there is no more pleasing sight in this town of London.

The point to which I should like to draw attention is that once these children of Saint Pancras are free born school and at the very moment when they should be encouraged to increase self-respect, the opportunities for keeping dean their hands and faces are diminished. To the strict individualist this state of affairs will not matter in the least. He will say that if youth does not desire to wash face and hands, then let face and hands go unwashed. "Who am I," argues the strict individualist, "that I should dictate?" Such modesty does not obtain with me, and I am much too selfish to refrain from interfering with my neighbours; besides, I know a good many of these folk, and I Uke to keep my own hands dean. The first grip counts for a good deal. No one is favourably impressed, for instance, by a damp, clammy palm, one that resembles something on a fishmonger's slab; the objection to dirt is in some of us equally acute. But to be fair, it has to be admitted that for the hard-up person the conveniences for ablution are not too sufficient. He can get a wash and brush for twopence, but he has first to obtain the twopence, and this secured, the temptation to expend it on something that appears more necessary must be great; few of us, placed in this predicament, would fed justified in squandering our entire fortune on soap and water. In another grade there are men who pay a subscription of ten guineas a year to a club for no other purpose than that of grumbling about the wet condition of hair-brushes; the folk of whom I am speaking consider themselves fortunate if their entire annual income is slightly more than this amount, and with them, the danger is that a brief holiday reconciles them to total abstinence. It would be the same with all of us. Mr George Wyndham wears a collar. I have never seen him in town when he was not wearing a collar. But if Mr George Wyndham went about Pall Mall for a week minus a collar, he would—well-dressed man as he is—find himself becoming reconciled to the omission; and what the hosiers and outfitters call neckwear would no longer appear to him indispensable. Once is not custom, but once several times repeated can become a habit. A few professions are exempt from the general claims of cleanliness; engine drivers are necessarily of a dark complexion, and even earnest reformers do not expect a dean sweep. Most of the tasks, however, which are given to a lad after he leaves school permit a fair appearance, and it is only required that the encouragement given in previous years should be sustained.

This is why I suggest to employers of hands they should provide good facilities for the washing of them. There are warehouses and shops and factories of my acquaintance where the opportunities are excellent; I know warehouses and shops and factories where the opportunities fall short of this high standard. I suggest to borough authorities—knowing well present cares sit heavily upon their shoulders—that they might arrange a set of taps in convenient quarters with an upper half protection, such taps to furnish a continuous run of water between (say) the hours of twelve and two, and the hours, in the evening, of six and eight. This free provision could also be made at the baths and wash-houses. A difficulty, I know, exists about soap, but soap is cheap, and can be carried in the pocket; there remains a difficulty about towels, but the best authorities are against the use of towels after a bath; and there is good ground for fear that a roller-towel might, as the man said delicately in "The Virginian," become too popular. Luxuries are not required and need not be given, but the excuse for going to the fountains in Trafalgar Square would vanish.

Possession of clean hands should enable men to arrest themselves, saving the police force the trouble of doing this for them. The grubby person is aware that the world thinks little or nothing of him, and he comes to appraise himself at a like valuation; the probability is he may put even a lower price upon himself, and as years go on nothing will induce him to reconsider. Near to middle age his case becomes hopeless. I never cease to be astounded at the enormous waste of good time and good nature given to imperfect maturity; if I had my will all efforts at amelioration made by any but the subject should stop when the subject has reached the age of twenty-three. By that period, the mind—whatever its quality—is made up; the owner of the mind can himself effect considerable alterations and repairs, but these are rarely made on the advice of other people. The weak mind is not influenced after this age; the strong mind resents influence. I would dam this stream, and, preventing it from going further towards the mature, divert it in the direction of youth. Efforts should concentrate on the juvenile, and voluntary efforts especially should be aimed at the years immediately following release from school. Also (as perhaps I have previously hinted), I would issue a garnishee order on the large sums that are collected for the purpose of pulling down a man's altar and setting up another in its place.

These are disputable topics on which everyone is permitted to have an opinion, and everyone feels sure the opinion he holds is correct; this is as certain as the fact that when the prime of life is referred to, it means the age of the person who happens to be using the phrase. To those who have been in the world for the number of years which suggests wisdom, I recommend the consideration of a means for encouraging clean hands and faces amongst the youth of town.

THE "GENERAL" QUESTION

The subject is considered unfitted for consideration by a mixed committee, and ladies, discovered in giving it debate, remark coldly, on observing the presence of an intruder, "We'll finish this another time!" diving swiftly into a question which can be understood by both sexes. If I am charged with impertinence in speaking of it here, I shall plead a certain right in that, having sometimes written in stories of an energetic, hard-working heroine belonging to the service, I have received urgent letters from housewives asking me to furnish at once either the correct name and present address of the young woman, or, failing this, the correct name and present address of someone bearing a close resemblance to her; to which communications one could but reply that an imagined maid-servant can only be satisfactorily placed with an imagined mistress of a household. I hope, however, the fact that I have, in my day, been treated with the respect given to the keeper of a registry office, gives some excuse for giving expression to a point of view.

Were I a girl, and an average girl leaving the London County Council school in a popular neighbourhood at the age of fourteen, disinclined to take any further rungs of the educational ladder, and with no special preparation for any special work beyond an accumulation of general knowledge (to the forgetting of which I should be looking forward with great relish), with a fair ability to use the needle, and, maybe, to boil an egg, the chances that I should become a general servant would be about four to one against.

The circumstance that everybody made elaborate attempts to induce me to become a general servant would cause apprehension; if (I should argue) the advantages of the situation are so great, why is it the market fails to obtain the excessive patronage given to other departments of labour? Wherefore, I consider the advantages of the dressmaking business, of warehouse work, of occupation in a factory. In these places there will be the prospect of companionship, I shall be in the movement of the world, my tasks and responsibilities may be great, but they will cease each evening at the moment I pin on my hat; on the way home with my colleagues we can be merry at the expense of the girl looking up through the area railings. She has some advantage in the matter of food, but she can make no brag concerning liberty, and any retort she attempts to the cry of "Slavery!"

will be hampered by the fact that she utters it within the hearing of her overseer. Supposing, for want of perfect health or disinclination for society, I decided to become a general servant, I should choose my first employer with great deliberation and wariness, striking out (first) the lady who had herself once been in service; (second) a small boarding-house; (third) a family with grown-up daughters. Accepting the most likely offer outside these exceptions, I enter upon a life of rising in the morning at seven, or earlier, and going to bed at night at ten, or later, and working hard during most of the intervening hours. I am called upon to wear a ridiculous cap as sign that I am not a member of the family; compelled to make my hands discoloured in cleaning boots and fire-places, and required to present them spotlessly dean before engaging upon other tasks. I am to show always a willing disposition, but this will have to stop short of vivacity; expected to reply to insistent remarks addressed to me, but these replies have to be free of the quality of back-answers. In a generous household one evening out allowed in a week— "And mind you're back, Ellen, on the very stroke of half-past nine, or else I shall have something to say to you!"—a half-day ticket-of-leave granted on alternate Sundays, this favour to be cancelled whenever company is expected; for any other absence, formal and timely application to be made. Right to add that in the same favourable type of establishment the food gives no grounds for adverse criticism, and at the midday meal on Sunday the mistress's remark is, "Cut off a good helping for the girl, dear; she has an appetite!" Wages, £10 a year at the start, and the lady, in handing over the monthly instalment, claims a right to be informed how it is proposed to disburse the sum.

Taking it thus at its best, the existence has a likeness to that of an inmate in one of his Majesty's establishments; at the worst, the female prisoner may, in making a comparison, congratulate herself. The points of difference here are really not considerable. The American in the story, who, looking out of the railway carriage at an arid plain, remarked that all it needed was plenty of water and good society, had to be reminded that the same might be said about the future world which some theologians promise to sinners. What the female prisoner at Aylesbury and the general servant at Balham both require to make their lives tolerable is increase of freedom. It must be remembered that the general servant is under the command of a woman who has no one else to command; all the slings and arrows which she receives are passed on to the maid, who cannot transfer the spite of outrageous fortune. The life is hard when work has to be done; it must sometimes be intolerable when work finishes. I am acquainted with a lady who objects to her servants giving spare moments to reading, on the perfectly true grounds that it fills their heads with ideas. But if they are not allowed to furnish their minds with the thoughts and inventions of other people, they crowd them with thoughts and inventions of their own, and when finding themselves, on rare occasions, free, they make haste to realise these confused aspirations. I have always argued that London proves a safe place for a girl, and that no one is more secure of herself than the average London girl; it must be admitted circumstances make the general servant an exception. One may fairly blame strict conventionality for the damage which strict conventionality sometimes has to endure. It seems a convention that a general servant has to be immured between four walls, and that when released she must be, so to speak, on the chain. Returning from an errand, mistress cross-examines her, demanding to know whom she has met, and seems to be under the impression that a right exists to receive the truth; small wonder, then, that when she does sniff freedom she should run amok. As this procedure is of no advantage to the world or to her, I suggest the time has come when a new treatment may be introduced. The general is short, and a world with not very good eyesight is apt to overlook her; if she were tall she would speedily promote herself to larger establishments, where servants are paid for at so much a yard. I suggest the world should put on glasses and take a good, dear view of the case of the general servant. She appears to me to be the foundation-stone of middle-class life.

The derisive title given by her contemporaries must be robbed of justification. The idea that she is a slave, that her body and soul are purchased for a few pounds a year, should go. The fact that she is a member of a great and beautiful country gives her the right to see something more of a wonderful spectacle on which, for her, the curtain has but just gone up. She should be encouraged to join girls' dubs, to mix with her equals, with her superiors. She has the right to receive praise, when praise is gained, and there exists no good reason why she should be the one individual to whom, nothing but blame is served. Where there are several members of a family the arrogance of command in regard to her need not be shared by all.

Having so far trespassed on grounds which are not my own, I am inclined to turn aside and to say, in confidence, to the young working-men of town that, in the opinion of one bachelor—a spectator, whose advice may perhaps not be entirely valueless—the general servant who has been considerately treated and to whom a wise and gentle superintendence has been given is likely to make an uncommonly good little wife. She will certainly be neat and tidy.

A PRETTY TIDY GIFT

In a clean, precise street of Coblentz, I once saw a man of a full habit reading a four-paged communication as he walked, one that seemed to give him no sort of pleasure, and having come to the end, he tore it impatiently into several hundred minute pieces, dropping these for a few yards in the gutter space by the side of the pavement. As the last fragment fluttered from his hands a spike-helmeted policeman crossed the roadway, spoke a few words of direction; the corpulent gentleman had to go back, stoop, and pick up each and every piece of the destroyed letter. In Tangiers—I fear this preamble is likely to give the impression that I am a well-travelled person; an incorrect label—in Tangiers, on the first morning, I went out early from the Continental Hotel, where I had shared the bathroom with a merry family of mosquitoes, willing to have a bite and a sup, and I prepared to go over the interior of the pure white town that I had seen in making the journey by rowing boat from the steamer. I told the hall porter I should return in a couple of hours; I was back in less than two minutes because, owing to some religious ceremony of recent date, the narrow lanes between the houses were littered with the entrails of sacrificed animals.

It would be easy to say, smugly, that we, of this country, adopt the golden mean, and sitting back with folded hands across ample waistcoat remark to the rosette in the middle of the ceiling, that we are not as others. The important streets of English towns certainly leave but little to be desired. In London, one may notice with them a weakness for intermittent surgical operations but this is a failing, so specialists tell me, general to the West End; once the wounds are sewn up, the outward appearance is watched carefully. It is in the less important thoroughfares, and especially up side streets that a want of tidiness can be discovered, with disorderly meetings of torn newspaper placards, hand-bills, jetsam of hoarding posters. Advertising helps to keep journals, and journals help to keep me, and I should be sorry to restrain the enthusiasm of commercial firms who desire to draw attention to the excellence of their wares. Also, printed matter of any description has a fascination and a value; I often wonder what the printers buy one half so precious as the wares they sell. The giveaway bill might claim to be harmless but for the fact that the involuntary bailee gets rid of his trust almost immediately, and with a good wind blowing, the handbill travels from Tottenham Court Road to Highgate Archway, resting at intervals, and everywhere contributing an aspect of carelessness and slovenliness; finishing the evening with some chance acquaintances of similar habits in a comer near to the line of yellow omnibuses. It is reckless distribution that has to be blamed. When I, a bachelor of middle age, find that the slip forced into my hand, is headed " You've got the girl in your eye. We've got the furniture in our shop!" the inclination to drop such a mental disturber seems hard to conquer. And as the German method would give me inconvenience, I ask to be kept free from temptation; I suggest the abolition of the give-away bill. The presence of so much Utter in London streets affects the habits of the people, encouraging in them the belief that tidiness is an over-praised virtue. I feel certain the methods of riverside folk have improved since the new treatment to which the Thames has been subjected; it is not so very long ago that the tide took up and down that stream a collection of articles of no use whatever to the owner, carrying them to and fro day by day, and never succeeding in ridding itself of the unprepossessing burden. In bye streets the wind performs this task of conveyance, and housewives, taking a broom, have no sooner completely cleared the pavement in front of their dwellings, and turned and closed the door, than the impudent intruders are back again. On Sunday mornings, when the world should be dean and sweet and pure, they constitute the one smirch defying cleanly habits of civilisation; the road-sweepers and the waggons of the Borough go home early, and when the carts are away the mess will play. In a Sunday morning trading street, business finishes at twelve and the stalls gone, the road is swept dean from end to end and a wonderful instance of conversion may be witnessed; but in the highways where no business exists the rift raff is allowed to accumulate, depressing the neighbourhood, and scoffing at reputable passers-by. The hours in question are reckoned sacred by the Londoner to church, or chapel, or bed; I feel certain that it would not seriously injure the souls of a few men in the employ of the Borough Councils if they were engaged to extend their services, and one feels certain their attention would improve the comfort of everybody else.

The dust carts are supposed to be for the purpose of collection; they appear to devote some of their efforts to dispersal; and it would seem possible that they sometimes return with a load lighter than that with which they start. Two men are in charge of the caravan, the lid of which, open at the top as it pulls up in front of the house, discloses the subscriptions from other dwellings. Whilst the wind prepares to toy with these, one man explains to the other that if old Billy Parminter had said just one more word to him the night before outside the Prince's Arms, he should have taken Billy Parminter by the neck—so I—and he should have punched him—so!—and he should have kicked him—so!—winding up by informing old Billy Parminter that civility cost nothing, and that good manners became us all. His colleague, incredulous, asks to be informed what old Billy Parminter would be doing all this time, and the first man, declining to be led into a side issue, announces he is ready to fight any man from Kentish Town, any man from Islington, any man from Pentonville, any man from Holloway, any man from Kingsland, any man from Hoxton; the other, interrupting, points out that he was born and he was bred in Pitfield Street, Hoxton, and the first man says weakly, "I wasn't so very far out!" and goes down to the area to give a thundering knock. As the two meet near the ladder set against the cart and empty their baskets in an indifferent way, they discuss wages, wives, beer, smoking concerts, and the wind takes the opportunity to scatter the lighter articles and send them back through the open windows of the first floor.

Wire receptacles in the parks and, in some districts, against lamp posts, have helped to teach a lesson, and the time may come when a consumer would as soon think of throwing away the fruit as the rind. We are not yet at that stage. Further teaching is required. A slang phrase is used by men out of work; they say they have obtained an appointment as Inspector of Pavements. It seems worth while to consider whether, in the interests of tidiness, a few uniformed men might be engaged to walk about, removing dangerous and disturbing and disagreeable impedimenta from the side walks, giving a word of caution to youngsters who do not know, to adults who know but, all the same, need a reminder, to shopkeepers whose interest in affairs stops at the doorway, and doing all this in a firm but good natured manner that shall avoid the extremes of Germany and Morocco. All the consequences to the people I cannot foretell with precision and detail—Shaving no great faith in myself as a prophet—but I declare no harm will result to their moral and bodily welfare.

The untidy habit of dropping aitches matters, in comparison, but little.

ACCENTS OF TOWN

A wistful protest was made a while since by the headmaster of a public school against the incursions of the Cockney accent, but having made a single effort with broom to keep back the tide he apparently gave up the struggle. For this one cannot blame him. Even with the headmaster of a public school life is too full to permit of time being wasted in fighting against overwhelmingly big battalions; possibly he remembered the story of the. father who, having swiftly prospered in business at Stepney, desired, in recognising his own accent was incurable, that his boy should undergo a course of treatment. The head of an expensive establishment guaranteed to effect a remedy in the course of a brief period, and the boy was sent. A fortnight later the father received a telegram, "Come and fetch your son away at once," and took the train cheerfully.

"Mean to tell me," he said to the head expectantly on arriving, "that you've bin and managed and succeeded in ridding my kid of his awk'ard 'abit of speaking already?"

The other gave a gesture of regret. "It is he who has succeeded," answered the principal. "He has succeeded in giving his accent to all the other boys!"

Every man, remarked Colonel Newcome, would like to come of an ardent and honourable race, and it is obvious we should all prefer to speak a pure and unadulterated language. But though the tongue might be willing, it is difficult to say where the type of correctness can be found.

I shudder to think of a time when all the folk in Edgware Road will speak in precise imitation of the manner adopted by (say) clergymen in Belgravia, and I ought to confess, before going any further, that the Oxford voice has the unique power of causing me to writhe with pain. Others I can bear with equanimity. The Devonshire accent is, to me, soothing and motherly; the Yorkshire accent sounds like a capital joke; the Scots accent means hospitality and candour; I should be useless in the House of Commons, for I never can contest any statement made in the persuasive accents of Ireland. The point is this.

Folk who come from the north of Berwick-on-Tweed, or the western side of the Irish Sea, are permitted to retain their idiosyncrasies of speech without a protest. Only the Londoner appears to be singled out and bullied into reform. It is true he drops his aitches, but why should aitches be aspirated? The order is not included amongst the Ten Commandments; it forms no part of our criminal code; there is not even a railway company's bylaw on the subject. A few years since people living west of the Wellington Statue decided to omit the final letter in words that ended with "ing," and nobody but Mr Anstey dared to remark on the circumstance; they were folk who had enjoyed the terrors of an expensive education with a rap on the knuckles when they said shillin', but they claimed the right, once free from scholastic control, to decide the matter of pronunciation for themselves; thenceforth to say shilling was held to betray the fact that you were indebted for your tuition to the County Council. At any moment this free and untrammelled set may decide that the letter "h" at the beginning of a word need no longer entail special exercise of breathing powers. It will be a great day for Lisson Grove.

An accent is something possessed by other people. There lives a distinguished musician who has the London tongue without knowing it, and tells stories illustrating the peculiarities. I have heard him give the anecdote of the little girl who said at the tea-table,

"Mother, can I have a piece more kike?" and received the reply,

"You shouldn't say kike, dear; you should say kike!"

The well-known musician, in telling this, adds, "And all the time they both thought they were saying kike!"

If a man suffers from headaches and is not aware that he suffers from headaches, he gives no order to the chemist; so long as we can possess an accent, and not be aware of it, nothing will be done. For myself, there exists a South London whine which always makes me think the user wishes me to buy groundsel, and for this note I have no affection; but to the other shades of the London accent one can always listen with pleasure. You find it at its best, perhaps, in Hoxton, where it is quick, sharp, determined; strict economy practiced, with words snapped out, repartee always ready. If I can do so without pretence of authority, I should like to make a protest against the methods of the printer in recording the London accent (impossible to believe the fault is with the writers); the ground idea appears to be that if you can but grossly distort the word and wrench it away from all similitude to the original, then you are making a phonographic reproduction of the voices of town. In a short story I have been reading, curate is given as "curick," "torked" is given for talked, milk is given as "malk"; these are deplorable errors, and I can only assume they occurred on the day following the annual dinner of the Correctors of the Press. In the same story I find the Londoner is made to speak of a Colonel as "Kurnel." I often see, in similar fiction, Tuesday spelt as "Tewsday," watch as "wotch". Is there any other way in which these words can be correctly pronounced?

I make an appeal on behalf of liberty of speech, as one who likes these identifying signs of birthplaces. A touch of the Midland accent, and I can see the Market Place at Nottingham with the cries of "Daffies, a panny a boonch!" A word from the southern counties and I can see a village cricket match of Married v. Single, a middle-stimip down, and, "Danged if that yer ball didn't upset his timber-yard, and no mestake, nuther!" A voice that comes from North Wales, and the valley going from Festiniog to Portmadoc is before me, with a shining stream making its leisurely way to the sea. I am probably not the only person who asks unnecessary questions of City constables, just for the interest of discovering, by the answer, the position of their county. Entire absence of affectation constitutes the great charm; a suggestion of the presence of this forces one instantly into a state of truculent animosity. Messrs Spiers and Pond would, I am sure, pay a better dividend if the young women who assist them in the serving of the public made a less resolute attempt to be refined and aristocratic. Any essay of imitation in any direction whatever is sure to carry one just a little too far, reaching the edge of caricature; and this proves well and good when done for the purposes of entertainment, but poor and bad when the intention is to impress favourably. Whilst we need not invent peculiarities of speech for ourselves, there seems no reason why we should violently rid ourselves of our natural manner, or why we should be ashamed of certain tricks of the voice which have not been deliberately acquired. The desire in some quarters appears to be to mould us all into one form and one manner and one speech, and this anxiety on the part of tutors may be understandable; so soon as their control is withdrawn a considerable freedom is exercised, and most of us are aware that the vocabulary of a public-school boy mainly consists of words not to be found in the dictionary.

In giving sympathy to those responsible for guidance of youths who do not wish to be guided, one may wish them, in all sincerity, a moderate success; to ourselves the hope can be expressed that the day is distant when the voices of all the people, boys and parents, will be identical with that belonging to headmasters of public schools.

THE PRECIOUS PARENT

The world shares the Wonderland idea that if a thing is said three times it is true, although, when the statement is one which opposes fixed ideas the number of repetitions has to be increased. Thus, a good many people, and many good people were contented with the novels concerning hard-up characters, stories which represented these as devoid of humour, sense or geniality; the reader felt that here was something dear, something obvious, something definite; none of your complex treatment, with fine shading and values given, but jet black. One was as safe in appraising estimation in such cases as one had been at the Princess's in Oxford Street the night before on observing in the playbill the name of Silas Throttle. That poverty involves cruelty was an assertion to which readers in those days would not have dreamt of giving denial. Old prejudices die hard, and occasionally revive when you think they have been buried, and it is worth while to call attention to a statement now made in an official manner, namely, that the over-whelming majority of brutal offences against young children is committed by earners of good wages. The parent in straitened circumstances may be careless, may show incapability, but you must look elsewhere for cases of downright ill-treatment, for cases of ingenious cruelty, for cases where pain is inflicted for the sheer pleasure of inflicting pain. In conducting the prosecution on behalf of the least fortunately placed children, it seems as well to refrain from bringing a superfluous charge against the hard-up father and mother that cannot be sustained.

Many a barrister, defending a hopeless case, has been cheered and encouraged on observing that the other side, over-anxious, has added one weak charge to six strong ones; he is aware that if he can but knock over this particular nine-pin, the jury can be persuaded that all the rest have fallen to the ground.

It may be taken, too, that although in this present year we are still being ruled by phrases, some have been found out, and we are no longer to be frightened and silenced by "rights of parents," by "Englishman's house is his castle," by "liberty of the subject." These are old weapons, not reckoned effective in modern warfare. Because they formerly terrified, we have been going on for generations in a silly, vicious circle. Thomas Grayshott, born in Lucas Street, Deptford, has a father occasionally out of prison, and a mother rarely outside the public-house until closing time. Thomas, as a child, has to bring himself up, and being only an amateur, does this badly. No one interferes to take the duties which his parents should perform, and Thomas grows with no chance whatever of becoming a reputable member of society; a fact that society later discovers to its cost. When about eighteen, the marriage service is solemnised between himself and Alice Court of Union Street (or not), and a year later a new Thomas is added to the population of London, to be similarly neglected by his parents. There seems no chance of arresting this persistent multiplication of disasters unless we decide that any parent who is not showing capability or desire to bring up a child correctly, shall be set aside and punished or fined, whilst the State does its best to stop the development of expense and trouble that indifference entails. Hitherto, it has mainly interfered when the parents were anxious to rid themselves of responsibility; I think it should step forward, in many cases, where the imperfect parent has no wish to lose the companionship of the child, and thus impose an additional penalty. Every child born into this world is a possible asset of considerable value to the nation that owns it, and this has little regard to the neighbourhood in which the child finds itself; as a matter of fact, talent and conspicuous service are being increasingly furnished by the lower middle classes. Now that efficiency is required in public work, the aristocrat can no longer be relied upon to fill every office. The instances, frequently paragraphed of Mr So-and-so, the popular Minister of Trade in the South Westralian Parliament, who has been home on holiday, visiting his father and mother in Horsleydown—these are good to read, excellent to consider, but I would rather Mr So-and-so had given his services to Westminster.

I hope it is possible to recognise the admirable work done under the name of Dr Barnardo, and, at the same time, to regret that the pick of neglected boys and girls of London is being exported to the Colonies, leaving the rest here to be responsible for future generations. If we are going to do anything for posterity—and I believe there is growing up a keen regard for coming ages—then we must give posterity a chance. We must see that infants are fed well and properly, and if their mothers cannot or will not see to this, then the State, at our expense, must become nurse. The public mind becomes impressed and shocked when an epidemic occurs, carrying off children; the awful mortality with youngsters under five years of age seems to be accepted with resignation. Easy enough to blame the parents and thus dismiss the matter. I have heard well-to-do women with no family of their own, argue with vivacity on the reckless improvidence of those who bring into the world, children whom they cannot afford to keep. A delicate question for open debate, but I have been tempted, more than once, to point out that even to the fruitful mother of Deptford, childbearing is not a lark, or a hobby, or a game, and that she, or any other woman, has done much when she has given a new little human being to the world; it should not be too much to expect from the world, some assistance later when and where assistance is required. The world ought to be grateful for its fresh recruit. It will, presently, drill the youngster; it need not be ashamed to assist it to grow up strong and healthy.

One temptation open to these parents which does not present itself to those more favourably situated, is the system of child insurance. We are agreed, of course, that brutality to children should be punished; I hope many will agree that carelessness justifies an increased interference. But I can see—I often do see—cases where a baby, being insured for a round sum, at a penny a week, grows up sickly, peevish, troublesome and the parents, being wanting in some moral quality, are tempted by the prospect of the round sum, and persuade themselves by ingenious reasoning that they are acting for the best in allowing the child to go. I hear the arguments.

"It's all mapped out for us. The poor little dear wasn't meant to live long in this world."

"He's saved himself a lot of trouble. Better off there than he is here!"

"We've all got to go, one day or other! "

It cannot be too much to ask that Parliament should find time (though this might mean that a few members should refrain from repeating a speech to which they have just listened) to make it illegal for an insurance society to pay over to the parents any money on the death of a child who had not been earning wages, but to pay the sum direct to the cemetery authorities and to the undertaker. I hope, too, it is reasonable to call upon the State to take up a position of greater responsibility in regard to neglected children who have the good luck (or the ill fortune) to remain in touch with life. I do not want to see the world turned inside out; I do not want to see the world turned upside down, but I do want to see improvements and alterations effected, and we shall see these results only when it is recognised that the young trees can be usefully inclined. The desirability that they should grow up straight is obvious; they will be in the way of others if they grow crooked, and seeing that we have a considerable interest in their growth, we need not consider too acutely the feelings of a neglectful owner. The probability is that the neglectful owner has no feelings to be considered; his show of temper can be endured or ignored.

INTELLIGENT MISCHIEF

The temper is greatly affected by the temperature, and most existing Governments are popular during the warm weather. Defiant processions have sometimes been arranged in London for a summer's day, and crowds assemble on the Embankment with sternly worded banners, and brass instruments of music that resemble deadly weapons, but once arrived in Hyde Park the wonderful expanse of green affects those who previously saw red, and the demonstration ("Certainly not less than 200,000 people," declares one set of newspapers the next day; "About 2000 present, on the most generous reckoning," says the other set), large or small, straightway becomes a picnic Only a moment's reflection needed on a warm afternoon to perceive that the world is a great deal better than we have any reason to expect it to be, and thereupon the spirit of rebellion either loses much of its strength or evaporates completely. A revolution organised during August would never stand a chance of success, especially if Surrey happened to be doing well at the Oval. But with the shortening of days, and lighting-up times becoming earlier every week, few can avoid the disposition to complain; faces in the street take a less agreeable look; mothers once more begin to say that children are a bitter handful. The State takes up a similar attitude with regard to troublesome members of its family, and in the late autumn an extremely common noun is used indiscriminately by magistrates and journals to any young representatives of the hard-up classes who happen to swerve from the straight path that can so easily be pointed out to other people. For the first and the last time in my life I write the word "Hooligan."

It is to the severity with which trifling lapses from perfect behaviour are treated that I wish to draw attention. One occasionally receives circulars entitled "An Appeal to Taxpayers," and one often sees posters with a like heading; they consist of tearful appeals to check the expenditure of public money on some clearly desirable object, and I am sure they touch the tax-paying mind, and tend to dose, with a snap, the tax-paying purse. This is why I want to remark that in the last recorded year we imprisoned at our cost and expense over a hundred thousand persons, who, their offences being moderate, were given the alternative of a fine, but discovered themselves unable to pay the sum at the moment. I trust I am not a mean man, but it seems to me I am called upon to pay a share of the cost of keeping people who, under the exercise of increased leniency, would be able and willing to continue the task of keeping themselves. A moneyed offender listens to the alternative without hearing; he has the cash in his pocket and he can pay and go free, sometimes putting the Court under an obligation by contributing a sum to the poor-box. But, in regard to the rest, it would surely be kind to the tax-payers to give the impecunious offender the opportunity of paying by instalments, thus saving the country the cost of providing him with food, care, and lodging. It is not a sport, this making of prisoners, at which any country need set itself out to excel, although the idea in many quarters appears to be that large figures mean good results. A chairman of the old London School Board once announced that all the numbers for the year showed a satisfactory increase, excepting those which concerned the Industrial Day Schools; he admitted later that, on consideration, this was not perhaps to be deplored. General feeling was well expressed by the incident. The average reader, on finding that so many more folk were punished last year than, in say 1896, says to himself:

"Good! Excellent! First-class! Capital!"

Adding, so far as one can judge the unspoken thought, "Hang the expense!"

The youthful offences which occur in the autumn and winter are variously termed crime or mischief, according to the station in life occupied by the offender. Highly respectable members of society, measuring forty-eight inches around the middle waistcoat button, tell me over dinner tables, with great animation and relish, of sparkling incidents that occurred when they were at school; of breaking into an unoccupied cottage, turning on the tap of the cider-cask, securing the choicest pears laid out on the floor upstairs, and when I tell them I have come across youngsters in the London prisons serving two years for gay exploits of the kind, they say in regard to their own adventures of years ago that boys will be boys; concerning the cases of which I speak, their definite and truculently expressed view is that this sort of thing must be put down by the strong arm of the law, and I am thus forced to recognise the difference between the choleric word and flat blasphemy. But why should the treatment be different? My stout friends received a punishment—

"All the better for it, my dear sir; all the better man for it; believe me!"

—And why should not the caning administered to him be the reward to erring youth given at Clerkenwell Police-court or at the Old Bailey? I know the terrible consequences meted out to those who say a word in favour of corporal punishment—the violent postcards, the fierce shower of pamphlets, the bite of the humanitarian—but I am not going to be stopped from pointing out that a birch is, at any rate, an inexpensive article, and the marks inflicted by it do not last a lifetime.

There exists a kindly spirit at the Home Office now in the matter of youthful offenders, and it is admirable to note the increase of common-sense and generosity that in recent years has taken place. The Home Office has, however, to keep in step with public opinion, and these improvements could not have been effected if the views of law-abiding people had not changed. It is surely possible, now that we have started a fresh treatment, to carry it further, without overstepping the limits of wisdom and discretion. I have sometimes been invited to read stories of London life to two or three hundred bright-eyed dear-complexioned youths, eager for interest and amusement—all prisoners. I have finished by speaking in a hesitating way words of advice, feeling as I talked that I wanted to say something, not to them, but to the folk responsible for sending them to the custody of the Governor. A few in such a large number are, I suppose, bad nuts. A few have determined that the breaking of laws is the task to which they mean to give their lives, and no treatment under the Juvenile Adult scheme or under any other scheme will induce them to take up any other career. But most of them are not bad nuts; they are only marred by a small speck, and I cannot look at them without feeling that if right were always right, and if justice were always justice, they would be playing at football in the fields close by, and going home later to the supper their mothers had prepared.

It is a sense of proportion which is needed. A small blunder should be met by a small correction; the enormous machinery of prison-life need not be set in motion because some lad finds an autumn evening dull and makes an effort to relieve the monotony. If, in this attempt, he acts to the detriment of someone's interest, he must be compelled to restitute, and the law can stand over him and see that he does it. But the luxury of seeing him in prison is to me so slight that I declare I feel disinclined to pay for it. One would rather buy a ladder to enable him to escape.

LADDER WORE

A principality which provides town with most of its drapers and milkmen has raised the chirping cry of "Wales for the Welsh," which apparently means a claim for perfect freedom of exports and stem protection against imported habitants; it has a peevish air of selfishness that will prevent others from copying. In any case one hopes that "London for the Londoners," although it might be considered a fair retort to Merionethshire, will not follow, and this, not because of want of robustness (a charge which appears to need some further evidence) but because of the Londoner's lack of ambition. In thus speaking generally, an injustice is sure to be done to many people, but it seems fair to say that the time and trouble given to the task of inducing the Londoner to increase his aspirates might well be devoted to persuading him to add to his aspirations. There are natural reasons why the immigrant shows energy and enthusiasm. The Russian Jew, arriving at the London docks, has, one may imagine, two strong feelings, one of relief in finding himself at a distance from a country that has not used him well; the other of keen satisfaction at the new opportunities provided for him. He takes the very first appropriate task offered, does not begrudge working hard and working long under a master, with always at the back of his head the determination to become himself a master at the earliest possible moment; his boys go to the County Council schools in Flower and Dean Street and, starting with no knowledge of the English tongue become free of the class for greeners (the new arrivals) in less than a year. London is for them the first night of a play in a perfectly new theatre. The lad from English comities brings with him something of this eagerness, although he exhibits it with more restraint. To take an unimportant instance, I came to Cannon Street at the age of about seventeen (having then been working for four years in a country office), and I remember how dear it was to me on the very first day that, in this astonishing town where everyone walked at three times the pace customary at Paddock Wood, and every vehicle seemed trying to pass others, and folk glanced reproachfully at anyone who arrested traffic by standing still—here it was imperative one should enter for the race without delay, and at once begin to train for it. Most new comers have experienced this desire to get into the stride of town and many, like myself, have, I dare say, gradually slackened the pace. The point to be urged on behalf of the London born is that they never receive at any period of their life, this useful and sometimes effective goad.

With consequence that the average Londoner, to whom the surroundings are ordinary and natural, is lacking in ambition, content if to-day is no worse than yesterday and willing, if it should not be so good, to accept the fact as a result of the inscrutable workings of Providence. He has a whole conversational book of phrases to support this view, from "Ah well, what can't be cured; must be endured!" to "You can always do without what you can't get!" This is the man who expects help from other people, and often gets help, and is quite willing the help should continue, taking an injured tone and a reproachful air when the suggestion is made that he should help himself. The pawnbroker makes fortunes out of this trait. The pawn-broker in response to an appeal agrees, that some misfortune having occurred to the prospective client, he will lend money on good adequate security wrapped in a brown paper parcel; the misfortune, by the law of averages, does not recur immediately, and you might say that the property would be reclaimed in the course of a month. Not so. The pawner seems never capable of catching himself up. On Saturday nights the package of clothes is taken out, on Monday afternoon it goes in again. He is always a week behind his income. In crossing the Swiss frontier where Central European time obtains, the traveller is able to set his watch an hour forward; a similar scheme, extended, appears to be the only possible means of enabling the pawner to get level. In a superior class, the townsman has no weakness in the direction of thrift. A city man earning a definitely fixed income permits his wife to spend nearly every penny of his month's wages in the early half of the month, so that when the days get into the twenties, a state of something like penury exists at Denmark Hill and father has to depend for public news on the placards and conversation overheard in the railway carriage; on the first of the month they talk about a children's party, and book two balcony seats at His Majesty's Theatre. The city can give examples of ambition and success, and frequently does this in after-dinner speeches; a certain reticence is exhibited in regard to the opposite instances. One need not agree with all that has been said in regard to the alleged dreariness of a clerk's life; many men are excellently fitted to be clerks and not very well furnished for any other occupation and their days pursue an even tenour which some, burdened with responsibility and the necessity for alert invention, may envy.

But one can admit that this steady, dingdong career does tend to make ambition wilt and wither, and that the features of passengers arriving at Liverpool Street at eight forty-five in the morning do not indicate hope and determination in the highest forms.

I can walk about London every evening of my life, and generally I find something new and frequently I discover something wonderful; the circumstance that I cannot always communicate these things is the fault of the man who drives my penholder. There are districts of London, however, where I dare not go unless I am in particularly good spirits, and these neighbourhoods are by the riverside, Barking, some parts of Poplar, Bermondsey, a portion of Rotherhithe, the northern side of Vauxhall; in all of these life appears to be, not without incident, certainly not without interest, but affected with a grim, sullen hopelessness. The fetch-and-carry men are here; men who can apparently find nothing to do but convey burdens. At the best, it is a casual business, unworthy and degrading; at the worst, here is a life which the Society for Prevention of Cruelty to Animals sees that no dog is permitted to endure. It must be hideous enough for the men to contemplate; the lot of the women requires enormous perseverance, courage. There at any rate the grown-ups are, and there the grown-ups must remain, but surely something better should be in store for the children. That any youngster, after the State has spent money on him for nine years, should be turned out with little other qualification but that for running errands, or carrying parcels; that he should be catapulted into the world without having learnt that energy and hard work and intelligence must be used, only means that the State is embezzling our money and ought to be placed forthwith in the dock at Bow Street. Excepting in the mentally defective, there must be seeds of ambition in every child; these are not in all cases likely to grow without encouragement, and leisurely years or years making no demand on the intelligence after leaving school are fatal to them.

A ladder is provided for the London youngsters, but it appears to be useful mainly for those who wish to develop into teachers. I know a child who has recently gained two scholarships amounting to £130 a year, available for three years; her father is a cabman at Kensal Rise. This is good, and I have nothing to say against it. But I should like to ask for similar encouragement to be given to children who show promise in other admirable directions. The fact that they happen to be without the special trick of acquiring and storing (and producing at examinations what is known as book knowledge, does not mean they cannot become good and useful members of a great community. Adroit help might save them from Catherine Street, Canning Town, where the pay-day is an irregular event.

It can never be said too often (and it will not obtain credence in some quarters even if one said nothing else) that London, compared with certain other towns in the United Kingdom, is a temperate town; compared with four in my memory, a town of precise, bigoted abstainers. This is only relative, and the fact remains that on Saturday afternoons, be the day one of sunshine or snow, you can scarce elude the lurching man whose task of reaching home is made up of a series of escapes from accident, terrifying to everybody but himself. Providence takes an enormous amount of trouble over the bemused person. I have seen him cross in the urgent stress of traffic, and with perfect safety, from near to the top of Shaftesbury Avenue across to Broad Street and New Oxford Street, an undertaking that to the sober mind cannot be entered upon without thought of a coroner's inquiry. Apart from the interest which comes in looking at a charmed life, it must be admitted that occasionally the man who has had too much to drink is a clown in a demure circus, doing preposterous tricks which tickle the audience (the female down, you will observe, is never a success). The sight of a large, grave man suddenly breaking into the step of a lively dance; the spectacle of an undersized house-painter endeavouring to control and direct the lines of omnibuses where Euston Road meets Hampstead Road and Tottenham Court Road—these have the unexpectedness that can be easily mistaken for humour. Excess of drink generally creates an astonishing change; quiet people become argumentative, the solid become frivolous, the cheerful become moody or truculent; I have known dull folk, under its influence, emulate the behaviour of witty divines.

Giving drink its due, the admission has already been made that it does provide a holiday for those who stand greatly in need of one, enabling them to leave their troubles and take a journey into a region where a Commonwealth exists, where they are the equal of all, paying deference to nobody. The holiday is brief, and the return surely not altogether pleasing, but a holiday it is; a holiday to which the mind, engaged on monotonous occupations during the week, looks forward as an incident well out of the ordinary. Large manufactories, where no man constructs the whole and complete article, but each does in a small way a small part, must take a certain amount of the responsibility. In some establishments there may exist a stimulant for the intelligence that prevents the brain from becoming jaded; prevents it from feeling the craving for Saturday afternoon and an event of magnificent proportions. The desire lessens only because London is increasingly providing other attractions; everything else being equal, a man would rather not have a headache, and he finds that, in taking his children out into the park to listen to the band on a Saturday evening he obtains a pleasure without any subsequent pain. There remain, however, the hours of Saturday afternoon. Saturday afternoons are not always fine—I claim no superior powers of observation in recording this—but when free from wet the hours are, to the youthful, easy of disposal. The youthful can storm the earliest tramcar or train, reach home, change clothes, and go out immediately afterwards to engage upon sport, or adopt the easier task of looking on at sport; to these it is a matter for extreme and acute regret Saturday occurs only once a week; on that day subject matter for conversation during the ensuing days can be collected and stored. For the veteran—the man of (say) over thirty five—the case is different. If he were in a better position of life he could go to Raynes Park or Totteridge and improve his handicap; golf is a good many miles away from his environments, and the game of bowls does not always appeal to a man whose back has been bent throughout the week of work. If he needed rest, he could stroll to St James's Street and, in the dub window, express views concerning the Government. As it is, he adopts the conveniently similar course, and puts shoulders against the swinging door of a public house. But he is not the only person concerned. Outside factories and workshops on this pay-day, you will see women-folk and children waiting, and in looking at their eager, nervous features, you may wonder whether something cannot be done to avoid middlemen's profits, to give relief to the over-worked cash register of the public-house. They want the money to lay out to the best of their ability (I have said the London woman is often an infant at shopping), they need nearly every penny that the house may run on endurable lines and pay its way. Several (this too has been hinted), have lost seven days of their financial lives, and appear to have given up all hope of recovering it; the missing week being condoned and arranged with the help of a tradesman, at a cost that gives to money-lenders in Vigo Street a twinge of acute envy. This they regard as inevitable; to be in a position where one abstained from a transfer of parcels on Saturday night and again on Monday morning might lay one open to the horrid accusation of thriftiness. But on the Saturday afternoon it is a life-and-death struggle to obtain a hold of wages before they are dispersed. Ingenuity, alertness, diplomacy are required. Every dodge on the board has to be used. Success is not 80 frequent as to cease to be notable.

In the interests of women who struggle, here comes a recommendation to employers of labour. Old prejudices die hard, and to send to the bank on Saturday morning for a bag of money and pay it out immediately before the hands go away to an idle afternoon, has become a form of ritual. "Always has been!" is the reply generally given when one speaks of the matter to the individual, and the immense force of this stubborn argument is known to all. Always has been; therefore, always must be. To-morrow should be satisfied to be as yesterday. "Once you begin to interfere," the same contention goes on, "with the existing state of things, you find yourself in a greater muddle than ever"; and this applies equally to a scheme for making the sun rise in the west or to one for removing dock-leaves from lawns. All the same, I submit that wages need no longer be paid on Saturday afternoons; instead, the payments should be made on Friday evenings. Certain railway companies pay on Thursday evenings, and this, with their officers and servants, answers well, but in the case of less reasonable men the interval might be too long, and the cash has to last long enough to reach the important event of Sunday dinner. Payment on Friday evening would give the housewife opportunity for deliberate shopping during the following day, thus evading the crowded rush which now takes place on Saturday evenings; it should interfere usefully with the men's spacious Saturday afternoon. When a certain pill was being introduced into Austria, the agent of the London firm carefully translated the long list of ills and grievances for which it had long claimed to be a certain remedy; he added at the foot that if any complaints existed in Austria which were unknown in England, the pills would cure them also. It need not be claimed for this small reform that it is going to be a panacea; but I urge it has the advantage of simplicity, that it can do no harm and may effect good. I ask considerate employers to gain the thanks of women, whose life is monotonous and hard, by giving the experiment a fair trial.

DAYS THAT RESEMBLE

A boy's first day at work after leaving school must always be a magnificent event, and whether he meets it with seriousness or with a light heart he will never, throughout his career, forget the details. By some misapprehension I happened to be invited the other evening to a party of successful men (I think, now, that perhaps I was intended to play audience), and these competed in early reminiscences, with special reference to the sum per week earned at starting; the award went, before a new competition—one on the hungriest moments ever experienced—was begun, to a Brook Street, Grosvenor Square man, who at twelve years gained four shillings a week and gave three-and-nine of this to his mother. The pleasures of retrospection in cases of the kind are understandable; I can always listen to the self-made man, providing he does not play golf. What I discover is that people who have triumphed took the earliest opportunity of getting away from work which demanded the plodding habit, from work where one day almost precisely resembled another. Discontented with the slowness of the march, they stepped out of the ranks and started to run.

One of the regrettable signs of life to-day is the gradual disappearance of the interesting side of work. A lad brought up on "Self-Help by Samuel Smiles, with Illustrations of Character and Conduct," may well imagine that life is governed by a fairy wand bound, sooner or later, to touch his shoulder; he finds himself, in effect, placed at an office desk where the first lessons impressed upon him are lessons of regularity, precision, cautiousness; no fresh methods to be tried or even suggested, and the one acceptable excuse for any action that of precedent. Thus, whilst still a recruit, he receives raps over the knuckles whenever he attempts to exercise individuality, and for answer to

"But what I thought, sir, was—" comes the caustic, "Jackson, you're not paid to think; you're paid to do!" Young Jackson gradually becomes reconciled, and, under discipline, ceases to be a human being, converts himself into a machine, a machine that hopes by driving a pen at a rate which never varies to reach eventually the maximum of £200 a year. In workshops the life of the youngster can be even more deliberate and exact. He will be set to do a small service in a definite way, and so long as he keeps within the narrow confines chalked out for him he is credited with sobriety; the time comes when he could do it with eyes shut, standing on one foot, a hand tied behind him. He discovers on promotion that any attempt to put energy into work and give to the day a special note is considered a grave offence; an essay made to exceed the usual limit, and the reprimands addressed to him by colleagues cannot be charged with ambiguity.

In the occasional occupations, there exists the element of chance and change, but the life, if merry, is short. These occupations are responsible for the unemployed adult, and furnish a reason for the extreme difficulty of dealing with him. A lad leaving school in (say) Lambeth has no difficulty in obtaining at once a berth which pays him about seven shillings a week. He may become van-boy or messenger, or he may sell newspapers in the streets, or he may sweep out a shop, and guard the front of the establishment; the work has incident and occurrences. This comes at the age of fourteen. In two or three years, at the very moment when he is on the edge of becoming a man, his desire for increased wages meets prompt dismissal and the engagement of a new fourteen-year-old to take his place. He is in the street, planted there, and the only art he has gained is the art of fetching and carrying. You will find him eventually either outside the wharf-gates below London Bridge, or he may be pointed out to you as a difficult subject by a deputy Governor.

The ridiculous part of the whole business is that during nine years the State has been spending about £7 per annum on the task of making him an intelligent chap, stimulating any reticent desires for general improvement, and at the moment this ceases and the headmaster has shaken hands with him and wished him good luck, the world applies itself with enthusiasm to the task of destroying all sense of ambition. He may bring interest to the simple tasks set before him, but of this he has but a limited stock, and it soon becomes exhausted. He may have hot desire to excel, but a cold spray of discouragement extinguishes the fire. In scarcely any occupation of to-day, carried on in the large, can he gain the content that arrives to a creator of a complete piece of work. If it were possible to exaggerate in the printed word the deplorable results I declare I would do so, in the hope of giving to public opinion the shock necessary before public opinion gives a cry or a scream. All that it seems possible to do is to ask you, ladies and gentlemen who have no anxiety to see the world grow dull and stupid, to give your encouragement and patronage to handicrafts such as certain cabinet-work, spinning, weaving, embroidery, work in leather, and so on, into which the individual has had the chance of putting something of his brain. I beg you to make a note of this in your memory.

As matters stand, and as events are moving, work is becoming such a monotonous, uninteresting, and automatic proceeding that the wonder is anybody possessing average intelligence cares to take part in it, or, being forced by circumstances, does so without a feeling of degradation. This feeling, probably, does come to many at times, and they have to decide between the policy of resigning their berth and that of becoming resigned to their berth. In the lower grades a third alternative presents itself. A friend of mine, who now has a stall in Pitfield Street, Hoxton, and is doing fairly well, informs me that he took this third choice, and asserts that, looking back, he does not regret it; only an injury to the wrist caused him to give up the profession—the right wrist, too, which made it the more unfortunate. Shy of telling of many of the circumstances of his career he, in regard to one which he considers the most sparkling and the most satisfactory, gives a full account. What do I say (the story begins), what do I say to four watches being taken, within the space of three months, from one and the same gentleman? The required ejaculation of incredulity furnished, the account goes on. "Picture to yourself, my lad, the Poultry, this end of Cheapside. Rather a portly gent comes out of his office there at five o'clock to the very minute, crosses the road; half-way across, makes a practice of glancing up at a very pretty girl typewriting at a window. I touches him for his gold watch. A month passes by; I stroll down there again. Five o'clock, out comes portly gent; half-way across peeps up at very pretty girl; I touches him for a second gold watch. I leaves him be for six weeks, and goes down there again. Five o'clock, portly gent, comer of his eye up at pretty girl; I touches him for a gold watch once more. Is that all right, or isn't it all right?" I point out a slight discrepancy in figures; at the beginning he mentioned four; he has given particulars accounting for only three. "Quite correct, my lad; I did take four. Four I took. Four was the total number. But the fourth was a Waterbury, and I put it back."

My friend has spent nineteen years in prison; this he mentions lightly, as we should talk of waiting nineteen minutes for a train at Paddington. With the exception of the injury to his wrist he complains of nothing, and, really, if you stand back and compare his life with that of a man who for thirty shillings a week spends the days in some occupation that never knows variety, never experiences change, you may find it difficult, as I find it difficult, to give him either reproof, advice, or sympathy.

AS IN '89

"The storm," says the history book of school days which bears on the front page my name, a fierce threat to possible borrowers, and a date which I decline to quote, "the storm spread far and wide over Continental Europe, and beat strongly though harmlessly, against our island shores." It is just possible that insular prejudice was responsible for the aloofness with which we, in 1789, viewed the French Revolution; a feeling that anything of foreign origin was, of a necessity, wrong and unworthy of imitation by Great Britain. At that time, the South Eastern Railway did not take a passenger from Charing Cross at ten in the morning and, with the help of the Chemin de fer du Nord drop him on the low platform in Paris six o'clock the same day, for a sum of twenty two and nine. In that year, we had as much personal knowledge of the inhabitants of Paris as we now have of the residents of Teheran. To the large majority of English folk, Paris must have been a little round spot on the globes near windows in preparatory schools, and nothing else; the town was probably never discussed, even amongst those who had its acquaintance, until the ladies had left the table. Folk having made the journey and returned were entitled to speak at length on the subject, and fellow passengers of Mr Jarvis Lorry in the Dover Mail (stopped by Jerry's hoarse voice at the top of Shooter's Hill with the message "Wait at Dover for Mam'selle") doubtless talked of the incident at every dinner to which they were asked for the rest of their lives. We are on easier and friendlier terms now with the Paris capital, and though London might not emulate any explosive incident which took place there, we could scarcely escape the feeling that it was occurring in a neighbouring city.

Little reason, however, exists for considering a revolution as exclusively an article of Paris; it is conceivable that it might be manufactured in London. What are the chances of a beginning? What is the likelihood of the finish? The Sunday in Trafalgar Square happened a long time ago and some of the leaders in that rather serious affray have advanced to high positions either in the State or in the Arts; others, of whom we hear less, are, it may be assumed, industrious letter writers in the lodging-houses managed by the County Council. Since that date there have been processions with banners of a startling nature, and martial airs of an even more terrifying description, but the newspapers have always been able to close their reports with the sentence, "The proceedings from start to finish were orderly in the extreme." Reasons can be found for this. First, the shrewdness and common sense of principals. Considering the number of words used in describing grievances, it is astonishing how few of them used in public places are either ridiculous or mischievous. Second, the knowledge that Parliament moves, that now and again Parliament acts, that any reform, generally desired, can be effected without the pulling up of park railings, or the smashing of plate windows. Also the very important circumstance that the disengaged Londoner is generally a lazy man—born so, or become so—and if invited to cross the bridges, or walk the length of Mile End Road in order to assist in a revolution, would straightway take to his bed. Nevertheless, '89 might re-occur in London and it is worth while to consider whence, in that case, the most dangerous recruits would come; what, in that case, would be the difficulties encountered.

A number of brisk pens have denounced the parade of wealth, and comic suppers at the Savoy costing ludicrous sums have been reproved. What wonder, say the brisk pens, that the hard-up people of London are discontented when they see expended on a single course that which would keep them in comfort for a year? This is a good theoretical argument. The hard-up would be justified in taking up this attitude. No one would blame them for doing so. But, as a fact, this view rarely occurs, and the further assumption that envy is felt is still wider off the mark. Canrobert Street, Bethnal Green, E. may experience something like jealousy in contemplating Cambridge Road, E. and the small shops in that modest thoroughfare, but it has no sensation of the kind in regard to Park Lane, W.; indeed, Canrobert Street is rather sorry for the very wealthy, and frequently says, in its outspoken way, that under no consideration whatever would it undertake the duties of Royalty. Those who desire to see an improvement in certain classes of London, and work daily with that end in view, find their efforts continually arrested and baulked by the fact that the classes in question have no anxiety for improvement, or for any alteration in their surroundings. They do not want to move. Enough for them if to-day is not much worse than yesterday, and if they think of to-morrow they are content that it should promise to have some likeness to to-day. This is not an attitude of sullenness; it is resignation, perhaps, it is certainly indolence. One can see them receiving news of a proposed revolution, and one can hear them advancing a dozen good and sufficient arguments for postponing to an indefinite date.

If I were entrusted with the task of organising a London revolution—fortunately I should not be the first man to be approached—I can foresee some anxious moments. I might go to Soho, and work up through the western side of Tottenham Court Road for there in the foreign quarter encouragement should be found, and perhaps enthusiasm. I might take a Wormwood Scrubbs omnibus and try Notting Dale, but the parts of Notting Dale I wanted to visit would require the company of a policeman, and there I see difficulty. Some streets off Commercial Street, east (foreign quarter again) might make good recruiting ground and I think one could get a few names from Brick Lane, Spitalfields. In certain of the boxing halls of Whitechapel and Shoreditch, gentlemen are found spoiling for a fight; they would want the promise of a belt or a purse. A waste of time to go down to the docks, and north of Hackney Road would result in the enlistment of only units. The florid orators of Victoria Park, and the public speakers near the Marble Arch comer of Hyde Park ought to hail the opportunity, but I doubt whether they could be counted upon for active service. There exists a dub in King's Road, Chelsea, useful twenty-five years ago, but impending Quadrille Parties prevent the present members now from accepting many other engagements. I should try the river on the south side from Nine Elms to Rotherhithe; the river, however, induces a certain leisureliness of thought, and valuable time might be wasted ere a decision was announced. The row of men who, leaning elbows on the parapet of London Bridge, watch the labourers unloading steamers below would probably strike at once for another twopence an hour. A few clerks not getting the promotions they deserve in the city, could be counted upon to desert on finding that their comrades did not belong to their rank of society.

Therefore, if invited to become the leader of a revolution, I shall urge that I am under a contract to produce a new novel in the autumn. The obvious retort being made, I may plead the time is not yet ripe, going on to recommend that no militant steps be taken until I have retired from public life. All the same, when one sees, hour after hour, year after year, the state of many of the less fortunate quarters of town, the hopelessness of the people, and their helpless condition, it is impossible to avoid wishing that all Londoners living east and west, north and south, bestirred themselves and announced a modified '89 in order, without scaffolds or the losing of heads, to readjust the situation. Meanwhile, there can be no use in pretending that this movement will come from within, and the sooner the fact is realised, the sooner it is seen that improvements must be effected by those who know and understand these people, without sharing their lassitude, the more likely the conditions will become a little better ere we write our last sentence, and speak our last word.

William Pett Ridge – A Short Biography

William Pett Ridge was born at Chartham, near Canterbury, Kent, on 22nd April 1859.

His family's resources were certainly limited. His father was a railway porter, and the young Pett Ridge, after schooling in Marden, Kent became a clerk in a railway clearing-house. The hours were long and arduous, but self-improvement was Pett Ridge's goal. After working from nine until seven o'clock he would attend evening classes at Birkbeck Literary and Scientific Institute and then to follow his passion; the ambition to write. He was heavily influenced by Dickens and several critics thought he had the capability to be his successor.
From 1891 many of his humourous sketches were published in the St James's Gazette, the Idler, Windsor Magazine and other literary periodicals of the day.

Pett Ridge published his first novel in 1895, A Clever Wife. By the advent of his fifth novel, Mord Em'ly, a mere three years later in 1898, his success was obvious. His writing was written from the perspective of those born with no privilege and relied on his great talent to find humour and sympathy in his portrayal of working class life.

Today Pett Ridge and other East End novelists including Arthur Nevinson, Arthur Morrison and Edwin Pugh are being grouped together as the Cockney Novelists.

In 1924, Pugh set out his recollections of Pett Ridge from the 1890s: "I see him most clearly, as he was in those days, through a blue haze of tobacco smoke. We used sometimes to travel together from Waterloo to Worcester Park on our way to spend a Saturday afternoon and evening with H. G. Wells. Pett Ridge does not know it, but it was through watching him fill his pipe, as he sat opposite me in a stuffy little railway compartment, that I completed my own education as a smoker... Pett Ridge had a small, dark, rather spiky moustache in those days, and thick, dark, sleek hair which is perhaps not quite so thick or dark, though hardly less sleek nowadays than it was then".

With his success, on the back of his prolific output and commercial success, Pett Ridge gave generously of both time and money to charity. In 1907 he founded the Babies Home at Hoxton. This was one of several organisations that he supported that had the welfare of children as their mission.

His circle considered Pett Ridge to be one of life's natural bachelors. In 1909 They were rather surprised therefore when he married Olga Hentschel.

As the 1920's arrived Pett Ridge added to his popularity with the movies. Four of his books were adapted into films.

Pett Ridge now found the peak of his fame had passed. Although he still managed to produce a book a year he was falling out of fashion and favour with the reading public and his popularity declined rapidly. His canon runs to over sixty novels and short-story collections as well as many pieces for magazines and periodicals.

William Pett Ridge died, on 29th September 1930, at his home, Ampthill, Willow Grove, Chislehurst, at the age of 71.

He was cremated at West Norwood on 2nd October 1930.

William Pett Ridge – A Concise Bibliography

Minor Dialogues (1895)
A Clever Wife (1895)
An Important Man and Others (1896)
Second Opportunity of Mr Staplehurst (1896)
Mord Em'ly (1898)
Outside The Radius. Stories of a London suburb (1899)
A Son of the State (1899)
A Breaker of Laws (1900)
London Only. A Set Of Common Occurrences (1901)
Lost Property (1902)
Up Side Streets – Short Stories (1903)
Erb (1903)
George And The General (1904)
Next Door Neighbours (1904)
Mrs Galer's Business (1905)
The Wickhamses (1906)

Name of Garland (1907)
Speaking Rather Seriously (1908)
Sixty Nine Birnam Road (1908)
Table d'Hôte. Tales (1910)
Splendid Brother (1910)
From Nine to Six-Thirty (1910)
Light Refreshment (1911)
Thanks to Sanderson (1911)
Love at Paddington (1912)
Devoted Sparkes (1912)
The Remington Sentence (1913)
Mixed Grill (1913)
The Happy Recruit (1914)
The Kennedy People (1915)
Book Here – Short Stories (1915)
Stray Thoughts from W. Pett Ridge (1916)
Madam Prince (1916)
The Amazing Years (1917)
Special Performance (1918)
Well To Do Arthur (1920)
Just Open. Short Stories (1920)
Richard Triumphant (1922)
Lunch Basket – Tales (1923)
Miss Mannering (1923)
Rare Luck (1924)
Leaps And Bounds (1924)
A Story Teller – Forty Years In London (1923)
Just Like Aunt Bertha (1925)
I Like To Remember (1925)
Our Mr Willis (1926)
London Types Taken From Life (1926)
Easy Distances (1927)
The Two Mackenzies (1928)
The Slippery Ladder (1929)
Eldest Miss Collingwood (1930)
Led by Westmacott (1931)

William Pett Ridge also wrote a play titled "Four small plays".

www.ingramcontent.com/pod-product-compliance
Lightning Source LLC
Chambersburg PA
CBHW021943040426
42448CB00008B/1221